ANTONÍN DVOŘÁK

ANTONÍN DVOŘÁK

ANTONÍN DVOŘÁK

by

KAREL HOFFMEISTER

Edited and translated, with a Foreword, by

ROSA NEWMARCH

GREENWOOD PRESS, PUBLISHERS
WESTPORT, CONNECTICUT

780.924
H67a
93211
april 1975

Originally published in 1928
by John Lane, London

First Greenwood Reprinting 1970

Library of Congress Catalogue Card Number 72-104275

SBN 8371-3946-5

Printed in the United States of America

FOREWORD TO THE ENGLISH EDITION

By ROSA NEWMARCH

MOTORING across the breezy, well-cultivated plains that lie between Prague and the Saxon frontier of Czechoslovakia, a league or so before reaching Roudnice—that interesting demesne of the Lobkovic family—a little village nestling in a dip of the land was pointed out to me as the birthplace of Antonín Dvořák. Nelahozeves lies on the bank of the Vltava and is guarded by an old keep, perched upon a rock dominating the river, which belongs also to the house of Lobkovic. Snugly enclosed by trees, it was a sheltered and prosperous little hamlet before the merciless requisitions of the Great War disturbed its peace and drained its plenty. But I saw it in the second year of the existence of the Czechoslovak Republic, and probably by now Nelahozeves is happy and prosperous again, for it lies in a productive district within easy reach of the Prague markets. On that exhilarating June morning, when a light cool wind was driving the silvery clouds overhead, and their companioning shadows raced them over the rolling expanses of the sunny plateau, I realized the unquenchable sources of sane and buoyant intoxication which

Dvořák tapped for his invigorating and simple-hearted music. His art was fresh and open like the countryside from which he came.

On either side the roads, which stretched like taut ribands across the landscape, the peasants were harvesting big baskets of plump, red-fleshed cherries. More than once I caught sight among them of the round-headed, kindly, benevolent, energetic and hirsute type to which the composer himself belonged. These men recalled my first glimpse of Dvořák, at a concert of the Philharmonic Society at St. James's Hall, in 1884. Some one sitting next to me called him "a wild-man-o'-the-woods," and he was certainly an unusual apparition on our concert platforms even in the 'eighties, when we were in the heyday of hairy musical phenomena. When we listened to his Symphony in D (Op. 60), which he conducted himself, the Pan-like element in this primitive being seemed quite natural, for the music surrounded him with a strong breath from his native woods and plains. How freely inspired, spontaneous and blithe it sounded to us mid-Victorians. The Furiant of the Scherzo carried me away, although I knew it not then for a furiant. We took Dvořák to our hearts forthwith, regardless of the fact that superior people had recently enjoined upon us only to swing censers before the altar of Brahms. Shortly afterwards we learnt that Brahms—so much larger-hearted than his disciples—had already given Dvořák his *imprimatur*. That saved the situation for "the best people," although, in the end, the not ungenerous patronage of the German musical world helped to confuse the issues nearly

as much as did Handelian tradition, and led us
to ask of the composer things inapt to his race
and genius.

Other and stronger symphonies followed the one
in D major, and into the conventionalized depart-
ment of oratorio and cantata the *Stabat Mater*
and *The Spectre's Bride* made bold entrances.
Only those, I think, who were already in the prime
of their concert-going days in the far-off 'eighties
can realize the extraordinary enthusiasm which
was evoked by those works.   But then, no one on
the sunny side of middle age can remember the
alternative novelties of that period : the flatulent,
sophisticated simplicities of Gounod's musical
" frescoes," or the insipidity of such an oratorio
as Garrett's *Shunamite*.   With each new work by
Dvořák we could look forward to something
joyous, and untouched by tedium.   Nor was it
only the general public which welcomed Dvořák's
music as dew in the desert.   The press was remarkably unanimous in eulogy.   His freshness
fascinated the younger party, while his respect
for form appealed to the older, more conservative
element.   Joseph Bennett was a fair representative
of the latter.   He was no indiscriminate welcomer
of new thoughts.   Although a few years later he
retreated rather cautiously before the incoming
tide of Russian music, in the 'eighties he went
more than half-way to meet Dvořák on his triumphant entry into English musical life.   The spirit
of compromise, on which criticism largely rested
in those complacent days, is evident in the following
judgment :   " Dvořák's success in England affords
matter for much congratulation.   We have from

him that which is new and not mischievous, that which is a legitimate development of form, and variation upon true art models, and that which is founded, not upon an elaborately devised theory, but upon the natural expression of a people's musical nature. The more of Dvořák the better, therefore, and the indications are that a good deal of him awaits us." [1]

Although not very clearly stated in the above quotation, both here and in other criticisms of Dvořák's music, Bennett shows that he at least was aware of the composer's national significance. On the whole, however, no one, with the exception of Sir Henry Hadow in his essay on Dvořák,[2] published some years later, seems to have taken the trouble to go at all deeply into this question. Who—apart from a small group of Slavonic specialists—knew or cared anything about the racial type so strongly embodied in Antonín Dvořák ? The Czechs at that time were ignored. Under the name of Bohemians they were frequently looked upon as the disaffected gipsy population of Austria ! If ignorance may ever be pleaded as an excuse for blundering, it is perhaps the only one we can put forward for inviting Dvořák, who was so completely a type of his countrymen, to compose works for which he was unsuited by race and temperament. We can imagine the answer we should have received from Brahms if we had suggested to him as a festival commission a setting of the Latin Mass or a cantata on a poem by Victor Hugo ! But Brahms was

---

[1] *The Musical Times*, April 1884.
[2] *Studies in Modern Music* (second series). Seeley & Co., 1895.

neither a primitive, nor particularly amenable to
suggestion ; whereas Dvořák was both. The
natural wisdom which led him to decline the subject
of Newman's *Dream of Gerontius* was not sufficient
to stiffen him altogether in the matter of works
made to order. If it is impossible to serve two
masters, it is equally impossible to serve two
countries. In the choice of Vrchlicky's *St. Ludmila*
Dvořák had at the back of his mind a British festival
work which would not be wasted on his own com-
patriots. In the treatment of a subject not
specially interesting to the English public he made
a serious—although perhaps not altogether an
irremediable—mistake. *St. Ludmila* is an attempt
to do homage to two parties, and compromise is
apt to endanger vitality, at least in a work of art.
Personally I do not regard *St. Ludmila* as a failure,
although it marked the first cooling off of our
enthusiasm for the composer. Looking through
it recently, after a long interval of semi-forgetful-
ness, I found it quite as effective as many of the
choral revivals of the last twenty-five years. It
is the most diffuse of Dvořák's choral works—
possibly he wrote to this gigantic scale in order to
please the taste of the English public which had
recently shown favour to *The Redemption* and
Mors et Vita ; but it has a certain indelible colour
and vitality, so that if the curtain of oblivion were
to be drawn aside, it would disclose something
more than a washed-out fresco. The most serious
drawback to *St. Ludmila,* as it is with most of
Dvořák's choral works, is the poor quality of the
English translation. Both Erben and Vrchlicky
were poets, although not perhaps of the very first

rank ; the Rev. J. Troutbeck was not ; nor was he able apparently to translate from the original text.

I could multiply instances from newspapers and periodicals of contemporary praise for Dvořák's music, but I cannot find any clear effort made by those who approved him in the 'eighties to save his reputation ten years later. It is significant of a curious psychological change in our musical taste to see how Dvořák's radiant and confident star began to wane as Tchaikovsky's meteoric genius came hurtling towards us through an atmosphere of pessimism which was peculiarly Russian. It seems now as though each musician in his day was sensitively prescient of the future destiny of his own country.

The decrease in Dvořák's popularity is not easily explained. There seems no reason for such a distinct reaction. With every ·composer, even the greatest, a wholesome and necessary process of elimination is bound to set in after the first indiscriminate acceptance by the public of almost everything he wrote. Our ways with music are the ways of the satiated owl with a mouse. But they are not so perfectly regulated, being a matter of chance rather than digestion. In modern life there are too many arbiters of the composer's destiny : the shifting taste of the public and the critics, commercial considerations, sometimes even the lack of a powerful patron to see him safely established. Too often it happens that the few works which " draw " are kept bright by use, the rest of a musician's lifework is arbi- trarily consigned to the scrap-heap. Even Bach suffered a long neglect. To-day we notice it in the case of Schumann, Tchaikovsky and Dvořák. Dealing with the last of these, I am not sure that the process of elimination has been carried out with justice. This is not a plea for the wholesale revival of Dvořák's works, but, after hearing in his own country some of the compositions that have almost entirely dropped out of our English programmes, it is permissible to wonder whether we have not cast out some wheat with the chaff. The Symphony, "From the New World," [1] some of the Slavonic Dances, the "Nigger Quartet," the "Humoresque" in its multitudinous arrangements —these are perhaps over-familiar to us. Certain 'cellists have had courage to keep the Violoncello Concerto in their repertory, disregarding sneers at its romanticism. But what of the things we rarely or never hear? If the Symphonies in D and F (Opp. 60 and 76), the Symphonic Variations, the Violin Concerto, the Moravian Duets and the Biblical Songs are too simple and sentimental for the present generation, Heaven help its complexity and dryness of heart!

An unaccountable feature of our attitude to Dvořák, who could once fill the Albert Hall with enthusiastic admirers and was cheered to the echo on our most important platforms, London and provincial, is the small amount which has been written about him. Since the article by Sir Henry Hadow, to which reference has already

[1] The great popularity of this Symphony is largely owing to the persistent propaganda of Edgar Speyer, who liked to see it repeatedly in the programmes of the Queen's Hall concerts, thus giving Sir Henry J. Wood opportunity to arrive at a highly finished rendering.

been made, nothing—as far as I am aware—has appeared here in book-form dealing with Dvořák's music. Nor, according to Professor Hoffmeister, is any rich bibliography of the subject existent in Czechoslovakia. The great, acknowledged authority upon the works of the composer is Dr. Otakar Šourek,[1] whose *Life and Works of Antonín Dvořák*, in three volumes, has only recently been completed. This monumental work, in the Czech language, will probably appear in due course in a German, if not an English, edition. But this must be a matter of time. Meanwhile the gap may be usefully filled by Professor Hoffmeister's shorter, but no less reliable, study of Dvořák's music.

Dr. Karel Hoffmeister, professor of the pianoforte in the "Master School" of the Prague Conservatoire, was a student of that institution under Dvořák's administration. That he knew and reverenced "the master," as he so frequently calls him, is evident on every page of his book.

Dvořák's life was externally uneventful. We know he passed through some moral conflicts when his Austrian and German friends would fain have detached him from the ties of his nationality ; we know, too, that he remained at heart a loyal Slav ; but, unlike Smetana, he was never involved in the thick of the political struggle. Unlike his contemporary, Tchaikovsky, he wrote few letters and kept no chronicle of his artistic difficulties and triumphs.

[1] The article upon Dvořák in the third edition of *Grove's Dictionary of Music and Musicians*, edited by Mr. H. C. Colles, is by Dr. Šourek.

In granting me permission to translate his book, Professor Hoffmeister left me a free hand as regards such cuts and additions as seemed advisable, having in mind that it was originally written in the form of lectures to Czech students, and is now intended to serve the uses of the English public. But for the amplification of the material dealing with Dvořák's operas, of which we are unhappily ignorant, and the omission of one or two references to polemical questions—of which we can happily afford to remain ignorant—the book departs very slightly from the original. It first appeared in 1924, in the series " Za Vzdělaním : Knížky pro Každého " (For Knowledge : Books for Every-one), published by J. R. Vilímka, Prague. The moment of its appearance in English is not inappropriate, since it coincides with the tenth anniversary of the establishment of the Republic of Czechoslovakia, and the social and political independence of the country to which Dvořák was deeply and touchingly devoted.

AUTHOR'S PREFACE

THIS account of the life and works of Antonín Dvořák grew out of a series of lectures which I gave at the Union of Culture, in the winter of 1917. The plan of my book includes a biographical sketch and a brief review of all his compositions, group by group : Symphonic and Chamber Music; Vocal Music; Songs; Oratorios and Operas.

The chief part of my essay is concerned with the features of Dvořák's work as a whole, with its purely musical characteristics; his invention, and the formal and technical side of his art. Moreover, I have attempted to penetrate the content of his works and to reveal their spirit. From analysis I pass to synthesis. Finally, because no phenomenon of art is entirely isolated, it is necessary to show the master's relation to the rest of the musical world.

I have laid special emphasis upon the relations between the art of Dvořák and that of Smetana. Also, I was interested in tracing Dvořák's influence upon his own period and the years which followed. In conclusion, I have added a few words concerning the school of Dvořák.

Were I to offer a survey of the literature of my subject whereon—as regards historical material—my review is based, it would seem poor in quantity.

The first attempt to describe Dvořák's life and

work as a whole was a seies of monographs
published by the Umělecká Beseda (The Society
of Arts), entitled *Antonín Dvořák,* prepared for the
master's sixtieth birthday (1901), but printed
only in 1912. The volume is rich in material,
but the articles—which are the work of various
authors—are naturally unequal, both as regards
their views and their intrinsic literary value,
while there is a general lack of unity. Many of the
features of this book—the outcome of its virtues
and defects—reappear in a similar enterprise:
the memorial article which came out in a contemporary journal *Dalibor.* Articles scattered
through various newspapers are fairly numerous.
V. J. Novotný, and after him Emil Chvála,
gave us remarkable studies of all the master's
works. In later years Otakar Šourek, a specialist
on the subject of Dvořák, has rendered valuable
service by his complete study of the composer's
creative work, including the more obscure years
of his life. Šourek has investigated the whole of
Dvořák's music, both in manuscript and in print,
and constructed a complete bibliography of these
compositions ; more especially he has settled once
for all the question of the confused and complicated
chronology of Dvořák's works. The first of
Šourek's books, *Dvořák's Compositions : a Thematic
Catalogue and a Chronological Catalogue,* was published by the firm of Simrock. On this authentic
basis I have been able to construct the whole of the
first section of this essay.

I have also frequently had recourse to Šourek's
Life and Works of Antonín Dvořák. This detailed
and scholarly book is based upon the author's own

deep and accurate study of the mass of material at his command. It is a book in which the author's completely equipped specialism, his erudition and keen critical acumen, appear on every page. Undoubtedly it is the greatest standard authority upon Dvořák.[1]

Before Šourek's book there appeared in 1914 Dr. Joseph Bartoš's volume on Dvořák. The author thus places the master : " the founder of our concert life—yes ; but no founder of our music." To Bartoš, Dvořák is only a musical exotic ; "and," he continues, " our national style is something far deeper than his sonorous exoticism; therefore for the sake of this truth we must be prepared to renounce before future generations even so distinguished a musical personality as was Antonín Dvořák." Here the point of view and tendency of Bartoš's book is made clearly evident. Bülow, Richter, Brahms, Kretschmar, Ehlert, Hanslick—all who were representative of what was great and serious in the music of the 'eighties and 'nineties — certainly did not share Bartoš's judgment of Dvořák. But of course he has not formed his opinion on their criteria.

Another and most valuable source by which to understand the psychological and æsthetic aspects of Dvořák are the works themselves and the frequent execution of them. In this respect the Czech Quartet [2] and Karel Kovařovic have told us and taught us more than the most eloquent words can do.

---

[1] At present only two volumes have been published.

[2] Long known in England as the Bohemian String Quartet, which only changed its name when the country became the Czechoslovak Republic.

CONTENTS

PART I
LIFE

PART I.—LIFE

IN describing Dvořák's youth and artistic starting-point, I base my book upon documentary facts established by Boleslav Kalensky in the Records of the Umělecká Beseda.

Antonín Leopold Dvořák was born 8th September 1841, at Nelahozeves, on the Vltava; the eldest son of František Dvořák, the local butcher and innkeeper, who was then twenty-seven years of age. Antonín's mother, Anna, was the daughter of Josef Zdeněk, steward of Uh-near-Chržín, in the district of Slanske.

In the simple environment of a rusticated Czech village, one of a poor family engaged in a continual struggle for the bare means of existence, the boy grew up healthy and high-spirited. His education, both general and musical, was carried on at first by the only person in Nelahozeves who was then interested in it. Josef Spitz was the old-fashioned Czech "cantor" [1] of the locality. He could play on every instrument—as his contemporaries bear witness—and was an excellent organist. The boy's attendance at school was obligatory for two years, during which he learnt from Spitz the ele-

[1] The word "cantor," as applied to the old Czech schoolmaster, is best rendered by the Scottish equivalent "dominie." He usually filled the post of organist and choirmaster as well as teacher in the school.

ments of violin-playing, and got on well enough to be able to assist his father in his capacity as village musician. Antonín sat with him at the second desk and took part in the "dedication festivals."

This is all we know about Dvořák's early teaching, for the records of the school and the oral information collected by Spitz's successor, Štěpán, were destroyed when the old schoolhouse of Nelahozeves was burnt down in 1885.

Towards the close of 1853, Dvořák's father sent the lad away from home. At Zlonice, four hours' journey from Nelahozeves, lived Antonín's maternal uncle, Zdeněk, at one time steward of the Kinsky estate at Uh-near-Chržín. This childless relative undertook the boy's further education. Antonín learnt German and carried on his music. He found a good teacher of both subjects in Antonín Liehmann, headmaster of the school at Zlonice. Dvořák continued to play the violin and also studied the viola, adding to these the organ, as was the custom with village teachers in those days. Moreover, he learnt figured bass, and something of modulation, besides "brambuliring," which was Liehmann's self-coined word for extemporization.

After a year had passed, Uncle Zdeněk called the elder Dvořák's attention to the fact that he might run his inn and butcher's business more successfully in Zlonice than in the little hamlet of Nelahozeves. He specially recommended him to take over a place called "The Big Inn," carried on in the house of a peasant named Novotný. Dvořák's father was the more disposed to listen to this advice because Antonín's mother was pining for her boy.

At first all went well. Later, however, the Dvořáks met with jealousy and unfriendliness. Dvořák's landlord, Novotný, would have been only too glad to carry on "The Big Inn" himself. In order to attain his wish he started drawing away the week-day customers to another beer-house, and on Sunday he lured the country visitors to another village. Thus the elder Dvořák came to failure and bankruptcy. Fortunately he had just enough left to complete his son's education in German, which at that time was absolutely indispensable. He sent Antonín for a year to a German village, České Kamenice, to live in the family of a miller named Ohm, whose son the Dvořáks took in exchange in order that he might learn the Bohemian language.

The choirmaster of St. Jacob's church at Kamenice continued to develop Dvořák's musical talents. At this time the boy acted frequently as his teacher's competent substitute. His former master, Liehmann, pointed out that it would be advisable to send Antonín to Prague, and the youth himself continually longed to go there. But it was decided otherwise. His father could not afford it. "It is impossible," he told his son; "you must be a butcher and succeed to your grandfather's trade."

A butcher's apprentice he became; yet there was no estranging young Dvořák from music. He occasionally took his teacher's place at the organ, and in Liehmann's orchestra, in church or at dances, he sat at the first desk, or still more fre-

quently took part with the violas, his favourite
instrument. In these surroundings the best
elements in Czech rural music were combined.
He found a capable teacher, and music, which,
though it sprang from the people, was combined
with the music of the country squires and the
residents of the castle. The old Czech " cantor "
provided the first sap of art which remained
latent in the subconscious mind of the future
artist. We shall see later that none of these
experiences were lost. It is said that at this time
Dvořák occasionally composed for the orchestra,
but put his works away because they were too
difficult. Heaven knows what became of them!
They are lost to posterity.

Meanwhile Liehmann, who was very unwilling
that his best pupil should be wasted as a butcher
and village musician, constantly harped on his
idea of getting the youth to Prague. The Organ
School was the ideal goal of both teacher and
pupil. Because Dvořák's father lacked means
rather than goodwill, Liehmann first approached
the childless Uncle Zdeněk. After a year spent at
the butcher's block, Dvořák's fate was decided.
His uncle promised help ; his father gave consent.
In the autumn of 1857, the peasant Veselý gave
father and son a lift to Prague in his hay-cart.
They stayed in Hus Street at " The Bee Inn."

The young organist lived at first with his cousin
Paní Pleva. He had other relatives in Prague,
among them his father's sister, Josefa, married
to a Dušík, who then lived in the Karl Square.
The Organ School was an institution which im-
posed a two years' course, and Karl Pitsch, a Ger-

man, was then director. It was located at that time in the northern wing of the former Convict, a Jesuit monastery in Bartholomew and Convict Street. In the southern wing of the monastery, on the ground floor opposite the present hall, lived for many years Professor Josef Leopold Zvonař, the chief representative of the Czech element in the institution. In this first year all the rest of Dvořák's teachers were also Czechs. He learnt theory with Professor Blažek, well-known as the author of the first good book on harmony published in the Czech language, and also for his vigorous defence of the use of the vernacular in this Germanized school. Organ-playing, young Dvořák studied with Professor Joseph Foerster, director of the choir at the Cathedral of St. Vitus; and singing, with Leopold Zvonař, famous as theorist, organist and composer.

In the second year of Dvořák's studies the situation developed unfavourably. The old director, Pitsch, died suddenly, and his successor, Josef Krejčí, was now Dvořák's principal teacher. Although an excellent and serious musician, he was narrow-minded and pedantic, suspicious by nature, and his character was uncertain. He openly favoured the German party at the expense of the Czechs. One proof of his lack of penetration—or perhaps still more of his bias—was shown in his undervaluing of Dvořák's gifts. The pupil whom he pointed cut as worthy of the first prize was an insignificant German lad, Sigmund Glanz, from Litomerice. Dvořák came second, and was described in the report as having "a good but on the whole merely practical talent. Practical knowledge and skill seem to be his chief aim.   In theory he is weak."

Dvořák's musical aims and tendencies did not move along the same lines as those of the very conservative and pedantic Krejčí.   But it is a fact that the two works which date nearest to this period of his course at the Organ School are a Quintet with two violas (1861) and a String Quartet in A major (1862), which do not conceal the influence of Mozart, nor of the masters who were later Dvořák's leaders—Beethoven and Schubert. Nevertheless, he soon turned to the romantic and neo-romantic school rather than to classicism.

Naturally he did not trouble so much about the theory and details as about the vital practice of his art.   In any case a great opportunity was offered to him by a musical society existing in those days, called " Cecilia."   Dvořák's classmate, Urban, says : " After the evening lecture at the Organ School we went every week to the ' Cecilia ' Society, which gave two concerts a year at Žofín.[1] These concerts, at which orchestral and vocal works were given, were famous.   Dvořák played viola in the ' Cecilia ' orchestra and sat at the same desk as Adolf Čech, who afterwards became conductor at the National Theatre."   This was an excellent practical school of orchestral playing.

What, however, was of still greater importance was the fact that Antonín Apt was the conductor of the Society.   This amateur was a zealous friend of contemporary music, an enthusiastic disciple of Schumann and Wagner.

[1] A summer concert hall in Prague built on one of the islets of the river Vltava, " Sophia's Island."

In this atmosphere young Dvořák felt happier than amid the conservatism of the Organ School. We do not know how far he understood Wagner as an operatic reformer ; but he was captivated by Wagner the musician. The neo-romantic seed disseminated by Apt through the orchestra of " Cecilia " grew and ripened in Dvořák for over ten years. He did not exchange the living instrument of the orchestra for the lifeless keys of the organ, even when, in 1859, he found himself in possession of the leaving certificate of the School, which recommended him as " admirably fitted to fulfil the duties of organist and choirmaster." He now stood at the forked roads of life.

Dvořák remained faithful to the orchestra. A former teacher, Karel Komzák, had resigned his post and salary of seventy florins a year to conduct a humble orchestra in Prague, which, in course of time, won for itself a good reputation. Dvořák accepted a place as viola-player in this band, and sometimes also acted as deputy for the conductor, who was organist at a lunatic asylum. Dvořák stayed on until 1862, when the Czech National Opera was opened, and this organization became the nucleus of the orchestra.

The agitated and strenuous period in the national life of Bohemia in the 'seventies coincides with the phases of ferment and the tempestuous springtide of Dvořák's art. Let us recall what the 'sixties and the succeeding decades meant to the Czechs. The reforms contained in the decree of October 1860 [1] relieved the pressure which, like a leaden

---

[1] After the failure of the campaign in Lombardy, in 1859, the Austrians made an attempt to conciliate the Slavonic element of

weight, lay upon the national and cultural conditions of Bohemia up to that time. Suddenly
the sap stirred in the desiccated tree of Czech life.
Spring appeared with all its hopeful indications
and promise of beauty. Social and artistic life
began to develop in new centres : in the Mest'ansky
(municipal) and Umělecké (artistic) Societies, and
in the choral Society "Hlahol." The first
national newspaper appeared, entitled *Narodni
Listy* (the National Paper). Literature found
leaders at this time in Neruda and Vitězslav Hálek,
who both worked for the formation of a genuine
national art. In the field of painting, Manes
laboured with equal power to the same end ;
while Smetana understood that destiny had
entrusted him with the task of creating a national
music.

Dvořák, silent and reserved, a conservative son
of the soil, did not let himself be carried away in
the vortex of fresh ideas. All the same he matured
rapidly in this new and forceful atmosphere. Of
course he came into touch with the new movement
though only through music. Not very sociable,
and rather suspicious, he kept within a narrow
circle. Among his best friends were Karel Bendl,
who was well-off and kindly, and offered him
assistance in every possible way ; Šebor, the
composer of *The Templars* ; and the ever-cheerful
Moric Anger, his colleague in the orchestra of the
National Opera, where he was afterwards conductor. Because Dvořák had no piano in his

the Empire, and Count Goluchowski drew up a scheme of reform
which, though it came only temporarily into operation, was the
beginning of better conditions.

Aunt Dušík's abode in the Karlov Square, Anger invited him to share his rooms in Havliček Square. Here he had an old spinet at his disposition. This wretched instrument was in a bedroom where, besides Anger, a medical student,[1] two other students and a man named Andel, who acted as guide to foreigners—five persons in all—had their habitation. Last of all came Dvořák, who had already a number of manuscript compositions packed away in his chest-of-drawers, among them his first Symphony, "The Bells of Zlonice," in C minor, and his second Symphony in B flat major, dating from 1865.

The C minor Symphony, which was only discovered by Jindřich Feld during the holiday season in 1923 in the musical collection of Dr. Rudolf Dvořák, has not so far been performed. Dr. Otokar Šourek in his review published in the monthly periodical of the Hudebni Matice, characterizes it as a work which sprang from a brain highly sensitive to expressive themes. "It is the work of an artist who has an innate feeling for all that is concentrated, ample and lofty in his art." Šourek continues: "Here, the later Dvořák announces himself in his handling of the themes as a composer who delights in the use of elastic, moving ground basses, and lively, sparkling, elemental rhythms." As regards instrumentation, Šourek thinks this Symphony is as luminous and distinctive as the score of the second Symphony in B flat.

This work is a fragment from the master's life. At the time it was written his existence was

---

[1] Karel Čech, afterwards an operatic singer.

3

indeed stormy and stressful. He was poor. The road to success was blocked and well-nigh inaccessible. In such musical circles as had power to arbitrate there was very little interest shown in his work. Some individuals, like his former teacher Krejči—now head of the Conservatoire— were prejudiced and unjust. He was also beset by love, despair and hopeless dreams; but he cherished an obstinate faith in himself and the will to conquer.

This frame of mind naturally led Dvořák further along the path of romanticism. He looked around for a poet who chimed with his moods in order that he might set some of his verses to music. Dating from the same year as the Symphony in B flat major (1865) is a cycle of songs, "The Cypress Trees," composed to somewhat tearful and effeminate verses by the Moravian lyrical poet, Gustav Pfleger. From the original settings Dvořák made a further choice in 1882, when they were published as Four Songs (Op. 2). It is characteristic of the musician's reserve that they bore no sign of being specially composed for his pupil and future wife, Anna Čermáková, but were dedicated to his friend, Karel Bendl. Again, in 1887, these "love songs" were arranged with accompaniment for string quartet, in which form they have been published by Hudebni Matice, in Prague, and revised by Dvořák's son-in-law, Josef Suk. Finally the composer returned once more to what may be called the journal of his courtship, when he composed the Eight Love Songs (Op. 83), published by Simrock in Berlin in 1888, with English and German words.

The somewhat motley company which surrounded Dvořák in Anger's quarters proved unfavourable for future work. Shortly after the completion of the Symphony in B flat, he returned to his aunt's abode. From his salary of eighteen florins per month he took courage to put aside two for the hire of a piano belonging to his tailor.

Of the music which originated in this house the greater part was destroyed. Among the compositions left after his death, not a single manuscript dating between 1866-1869 was found. Dvořák declared that he himself, " tore up and burned the works of this period." They consisted of two Overtures for Orchestra ; a String Quartet in B minor ; a Mass in B and—if V. J. Novotný is correct in his statement—possibly another Mass in F minor, besides a Clarinet Quartet in B flat minor. In addition, he also appears to have destroyed a number of entr'actes and other incidental pieces composed for the National Theatre, regarding which the conductor, Adolphe Čech, bore witness that they were remarkably symphonic in style.

In the spring of 1870 Dvořák entered a new field of activity. He now began to work on the opera, *Alfred*.

Undoubtedly the current of operatic activity, so vital in Bohemia at that period, influenced the composer, then twenty-nine. Šebor's opera, *The Templars in Moravia*, was first produced in 1865 ; the following year brought forth Smetana's, *The Brandenburgers in Bohemia* and *The Bartered Bride* ; a little later came Šebor's *Drahomira*, followed by his *Hussite Bride*; while Bendl's *Lejla* and

Smetana's *Dalibor* appeared in 1868. Moric Anger remembered that Dvořák at this time gladly and frequently accompanied him to the German theatre, where Wagner's operas interested him immensely. Seeing that all the most important voices among the Czechs, with Smetana as leader, were advocating Wagner's reforms, it is not surprising that the young musician, having raked up a libretto by Theodore Körner from an old German magazine, should try to handle it on lines acquired from listening to Wagner's operas. In setting this heroic northern story of the ninth century, Dvořák endeavoured to make use of typical leit-motifs, and sought for the simplest independence of the vocal parts in a declamatory style which was developed from the chief melodic current in the orchestra.

Otokar Šourek, whom we must thank for a valuable analysis of the work, indicates that the whole attempt was a mistake. Between much musical poverty and the monotonous modulation of the recitatives a few good and homogeneous numbers are interpolated. Šourek also points out the little scenes in Acts II. and III. as showing more warmth and animation than those of the first Act. *Alfred* was never performed on the stage. Only the overture, found and published by Simrock in 1912, under the title of Dramatic Overture, is important as a proof of Dvořák's early maturity and technical skill.

The style and ideas which inspired *Alfred* are also linked with the two String Quartets in D major and E minor, both of which are bubbling over with the leaven of Dvořák's neo-romantic and

Wagnerian tendencies. These and the Sonata in F minor—of which only the 'cello part has been preserved—stand between *Alfred* and Dvořák's next operatic venture.

This time he turned to a comic opera—*King and Collier*. That this work has been so long neglected is due perhaps to the fact that until recently the score was believed to be lost, or perhaps destroyed. Then Dr. Jan Löwenbach heard by chance that Josef Aupěk—formerly a member of the orchestra of the National Theatre—had purchased from a theatrical agent in Norimberk two bound scores which were recognized as Dvořák's lost manuscript. Šourek, who made a detailed analysis of the opera, which was written to a libretto arranged by Bertrand Guldener, declared that the legends circulated up to that time regarding the impossibility of conducting this score are actually as great an invention as the myth concerning its Wagnerian style. It is true that the score does not deny a direct connection with Dvořák's neo-romantic phase ; but it is evidently a great and decisive step along the composer's road towards a settled and independent goal. There is no obstacle to its performance on account of its excessive technical difficulties. Moreover, it is interesting to note that in his remodelling of this same libretto—of which we shall speak presently—Dvořák did not use a single bar of this first version. Only the extreme modesty of the composer can have induced him to withdraw this opera from its promised performance, which might have proved a significant event in the evolution of Czech opera.

In the meantime, however, while the critics

continued to admonish him with benevolent
patience, Dvořák was proving in another work
that he had already overcome the deficiencies for
which he was being blamed. He had a work in
hand—an expression of deep patriotic sentiment,
and a manifestation entirely personal in character
—which was to conquer at a blow. On 3rd June
1872 he put the last touches to the *Hymnus*, taken
from Hálek's lyrical epic, " The Heirs of the White
Mountain."

The first performance of this composition,
dedicated to Vitězlav Hálek (here observe the
musician's respect for the poet), took place on
9th March 1873 at the Novoměstsky Theatre,
conducted by Karel Bendl. The concert was the
first given by the newly organized, and now famous,
mixed-voice choir, "Hlahol."[1] This was the occasion of Dvořák's first great triumph. Even Ludevit
Procházka,[2] usually so severe to Dvořák, wrote
with enthusiasm : " The work seems cast in one
jet ; it flows in an unbroken stream of truthful
and expressive declamation, linked to animated
and highly coloured orchestration, in a richly
polyphonic form. It is in the genuine hymn-
style, clear-cut and sublime. In short, it is a
virile and eloquent idea, a masterly sketch, worthy
of the new epoch. A breath meets us here which
blends with Hálek's inspiration in a beautiful
whole."

Dvořák was not wholly contented with the
Hymnus. He revised it before it was printed by

[1] A word meaning " sound " or " sonority.".
[2] Born 1837 ; died 1888 in Prague ; a well-known critic and
writer on musical questions.

the firm of Novello in 1885, and partially remodelled it for one of the Slavonic Concerts in 1888.

Another of Dvořák's works, missing for many years, was ultimately found among some manuscripts in the Czech Museum. This was the pianoforte Quintet in A major,[1] completed in September 1872, remarkable as belonging to a series of compositions that reflect the clarity and orderliness to which the composer's art was gradually attaining. After its production at a matinée on 22nd November in the year of its completion, Procházka chastised it severely for its lack of formal polish, and pointed to the " well attested " form of its predecessors. Šourek explains, with greater justice, that we must attribute Dvořák's freedom of form at that time not to any lack of finish—because he had already shown his mastery in many earlier works—but to a distinctly conscious effort to find new forms ; to a deliberate revulsion from the fixed formal standard. " Thus explained, the nature of Dvořák's art appears in quite another light to that in which certain people have hitherto chosen to view it. The tendencies we have been observing are certainly not indicative of a profoundly conservative spirit which always adheres to a formal scheme ! "

The cycle of songs written in September and October 1872 may serve as a proof of how deeply Dvořák has been wronged by those who have laid stress upon his lack of literary culture, emphasizing that, as a composer, his attitude to poetry was

---

[1] See the third edition of *Grove's Dictionary of Music and Musicians*, where Šourek mentions it among the list of Dvořák's unpublished works as having been originally numbered Op. 5.

hopeless. Let us note the fact that Dvořák did not care to write individual, heterogeneous songs. He composed at this time two cycles : the Songs from Serbian Folk Poetry and the Songs from the Kralodvorsky Manuscript. The Serbian Songs (Op. 6) were composed immediately after the appearance of S. Kupper's translations of *World Poetry*. Dvořák must therefore have known what was going on in literature. Both these cycles contributed so much that was new and original to the comparatively small output of Bohemian lyrics that neither singers nor critics understood them. Even acute judges shook their heads over their excessive " modernity." The Songs from the Kralodvorsky Manuscript are interesting as being among Dvořák's earliest published works. This famous Manuscript, around which controversy raged for over a century, was discovered by Hanka in 1817, at Königinhof (Kralove Dvur) in the north-east of Bohemia. Its authenticity was challenged at once, particularly by the German scholars. In later years several Czechs, including Thomas Masaryk, now President of the Czechoslovak Republic, have helped to explode the illusion of its veracity. To part with faith in its authenticity is, for lovers of folk-lore and epic literature, a matter of regret, as in the case of the poems of Ossian, and perhaps also of the Finnish Kalevala. But, forgery or not, the Manuscript contains a few charming lyrics [1] of which Dvořák was quick to take advantage. They first appeared

---

[1] An accurate translation of the poems was published at Cambridge by the Rev. A. H. Wratislaw, 1852. Other English versions appear in Professor Morfill's *Slavonic Literature*, S.P.C.K., 1883.

in March 1873, published by the firm of Emil
Starý of Prague. Later on, in 1879, Simrock
reprinted both these song-cycles in German and
English versions, entirely omitting the original
Czech words.

Another work which had a great success with
the Czech public originated side by side with the
Serbian Songs. In October 1872, Dvořák wrote
three Nocturnes for Orchestra, of which the third
was given at a concert of the Prague Philharmonic
Society, conducted by Slánsky, on 3rd March, at
Žofín Island. The critics were quite as enthusiastic
as they had been a month previously over the
production of the *Hymnus*.

But Dvořák, the auto-critic, was of a different
opinion. He burnt the Nocturnes like so many of
his works which he himself ruled out and destroyed.
Perhaps this was also the fate of a violin sonata,
performed for the last time in 1875, and never
heard of again from that day to this. All through
his life Dvořák refused to send to the printer music
which did not satisfy his own critical standard—
even such a thoughtful and mature work as the
Symphony in E flat, begun in April and finished in
June 1873. And yet Smetana himself had recognized its value by conducting it at one of
the Philharmonic Concerts on 30th March 1874.
Smetana, of course, may have been in sympathy
with the neo-romantic spirit which permeates this
aspiring and pathetic work ; undoubtedly he would
have been in sympathy with a composition which
slipped so completely out of the control of the
commonplace, and from which Dvořák had weeded
out all that was likely to be most pleasing to the

critics of the day. The work was very severely
cut up as regards form. And it was characteristic
of Dvořák—who all his life kept an exaggerated
respect for the printed word—that although he
himself liked the Symphony it was not given
again during his life. It was revived for the first
time in 1904, after Dvořák's death, by Jindřich
z Kaan at one of the Conservatoire Concerts, and
published by Simrock as late as 1912.

In the spring of 1873, events led Dvořák into a
field of activity which he made his very own ; I
refer to his quartet writing. At this time a chamber-
music society of the first rank came into existence
in Bohemia, with Antonín Benevic (Benewitz) as
leader, Deutsch as second violin, Vojtech Hřímalý
as viola, and Smetana as pianist. It coincided
with a phase of yearning and meditation in Dvořák.
He longed to express these intimate moods of his
soul. Once again he stood at the parting of life's
ways—marriage was in prospect.

A month before this took place he finished a
String Quartet in F minor—originally Op. 29, but
later numbered Op. 9. In this work he surveys
his troubled and suffering past, and turns in glad
greeting to the new dawn which showed a prospect
of artistic and domestic happiness. Šourek points
to the biographical significance of this Quartet
which, he says, Dvořák, copying Smetana's example,
might equally well have named " From out my
life." The work remains in manuscript. Only
the slow movement, remodelled, and published by
Simrock as a Romance for Violin and Orchestra
(Op. 11), is accessible to the world.

At last, the parents of Anna Čermáková, who

had long been Dvořák's pupil and the object of his
affections, overcame their distrust of a musician's
earning-powers, and consented to the marriage,
which took place in St. Peter's Church, Prague,
on 17th November 1873. The young couple spent
the first three months of married life with the
bride's parents, and then found a modest, but cosy,
home in Prague at No. 14, Rybníčka. Henceforth
the composer's energetic and practical wife supple-
mented the qualities which nature had denied to
her husband. Self-assertion and practical common
sense were his weakest points. Dvořák's home
formed a centre in which he could now create new
works in peace. Naturally the rapture of love
found expression at this time, and once again in
the intimate form of the string quartet. Šourek
indicates the characteristic features of these manuscripts and unfinished works, showing how Dvořák
now tried to weld the customary four movements
of the quartet into one organic whole. He also
points out in his analysis how the musician—following other modern works—sought to be monothe-
matic, to give firmness and unity to the whole
work by means of one fundamental theme. It is
said that one of Dvořák's favourite models at this
time was Beethoven's Quartet in C sharp minor
(Op. 135).

These quartets did not, in fact, find favour with
Benevic's chamber-music society, but Dvořák's
faith in himself had been awakened by the success
of the *Hymnus* and other lesser triumphs. For
this reason he now ventured to cast off the thraldom
of the theatre, and in the year of his marriage
resigned his post in the orchestra of the National

Theatre. He now found compensation for the small salary he had earned as a viola player in the organist-ship of St. Vojtech's church. The organ as an instrument never attracted him greatly. According to Josef Foerster (the choirmaster of St. Vojtech's at that time), Dvořák's improvisations were not manifestations of outstanding talent. Janáček corroborated this opinion. He said : "Dvořák improvised hesitatingly ; Stehle and Witt wrote down the preludes to their Masses, and it seemed as though Dvořák introduced his in much the same style."

On the other hand, Dvořák, steeped in domestic happiness, penetrated deeper and deeper to the root of his own individuality ; without external prompting he now discovered his tendencies to purely Czech music.

We can only guess the paths by which Dvořák reached the innermost core of his being. He talked very little, and never about the inward events of life ; nor did he write a word on the subject. It is certain, however, that in the peace of his home, the experimental and analytical spirit, characteristic of his earlier period, now ceased to be active. He had discovered his guiding light, which had gleamed for him in times of dark despair, and now shone on him without setting. Beethoven and Schubert had shown him the way to express what lay in the depths of his soul. Through the influence of these masters he had found his most suitable forms. Now, drawing only upon himself—and thanks also to the impulse derived from Smetana—he found his Czech and Slavonic musical soul.

He offered homage to the classical masters in
the first great works of this period. The first three
months of 1873 saw the completion of the Symphony
in D minor (Op. 13), in four movements. Immediately afterwards, in the following May, Smetana
conducted the Scherzo of this work at the Novoměstsky Theatre at a concert given by the Academic
Society. The entire work was not given, however,
until April 1892, at Dvořák's farewell concert before
leaving for America. A critic wrote : " This
Symphony marks a considerable advance upon its
predecessors by its clearness of form and rich
elaboration of the themes, and by the expressive
ideas contained in it. The orchestration, too,
shows greater transparency and the tonal quality
is more beautiful." After this Dvořák returned
at once to the path trodden by the Czech
patriot-musician Smetana—the path of national
opera.

This move was not surprising. He had witnessed
the permanent success of *The Bartered Bride*.
The Brandenburgers in Bohemia and *Dalibor* had
both been produced. There was also *Libuša*,
although only famous at that time because of the
gossip about its extreme Wagnerism ; and again
in 1874 Smetana showed in *The Two Widows* the
possibility of taking a new line in Czech opera.
Dvořák certainly realized wherein lay Smetana's
force ; it is certain, at this time, that he understood Smetana's ideal of national music. He, too,
wished to take part in its development, and, like
its founder, turned to the operatic stage.

Already, in 1872, he had composed music to a
poor libretto (" King and Collier ") by Guldener,

and after his score had been sent to the National Theatre he withdrew it. It is characteristic of Dvořák's simplicity that he should have set his hopes on this text, based upon a puppet play by Mathew Kopecky It says much for his toughness of moral fibre that the moment he had completed the D minor Symphony he returned to work on the opera. Five months later, in August, the score was entirely rewritten, with the exception of the overture, which was only finished in November 1874, when the work was put into rehearsal at the Theatre. Josef B. Foerster, who was then organist of St. Vojtech, remembers how the choir were interested in the reports which came in from week to week, and were most reassuring. The longer the opera was rehearsed the greater the appreciation and admiration of all concerned ; there were rumours of wonderfully beautiful melody and of the dramatic vigour of the chief scenes ; of splendid polyphony and thematic development. By the time the day of perform-ance arrived, every one was aware that Czech art had found in Dvořák one of the elect among musicians.

After the first night, 24th November 1874, when the work had a brilliant success, Procházka wrote in the musical journal *Dalibor* : "There is no need to be anxious about Dvořák's future. The composer, after long groping, has found the right path to the temple of independent Slavonic art. . . . In future, Dvořák will liberate his work more and more from exotic influences, and with the triumphant future of Slavonic music the en-thusiasm of this artist will place him in the ranks

---

of those whose names will stand out in letters of gold in our annals."

It seemed, however, that the lasting success of *King and Collier* was to be hindered by Guldener's libretto. Vaclav J. Novotný tried as far as possible to eliminate its faults. It was produced in his amended version in June 1887, but unfortunately in a very careless way. After this, it dropped out of the repertory, until Kovařovic revived it in 1914, and Roman Vesely's pianoforte score made it accessible.

As almost invariably happened after each of his operas, Dvořák reverted from *King and Collier* to quartet-writing. His Quartet in A minor, which in form and matter adheres closely to classical models, was composed at this time.

Then he went back once again to opera. *Tvrdě Palice* (*The Pig-headed Peasants*) in one act, the libretto by Josef Štolba, was completed on Christmas Day, 1874, and offered without delay to the National Theatre. But seven years elapsed before it was produced for the first time, on 2nd October 1881, when the entire staging was so bad that, after the second night, the Director of the theatre prohibited its further performance until "decent and worthy" scenery and costumes could be acquired for it. The first night was an immediate success, but the work did not take a firm hold on the public until 1900. The pianoforte score was published by Simrock.

Added to these successes, the year 1875 brought an improvement in Dvořák's pecuniary position. From this time forth he prospered in a modest and unpretentious way, until, in 1876, he was able to give up his organist's post and live entirely for composition.

In 1863 a State grant had been instituted in Vienna for "young, poor, and talented artists, painters, sculptors, and musicians in the Austrian half of the Empire." On the recommendation of friends Dvořák applied for the grant, and learnt, in 1875, that the sum of 400 gold florins had been awarded him by the jury. This was the first material recompense for his work which had fallen to his lot—a recompense which in his humble position as organist was undoubtedly welcome. But it meant more than this. The musical section of the jury which dealt with this fund included Eduard Hanslick, critic of the *Neue Freie Presse*; Johannes Brahms; and the conductor of the Vienna Opera, Johann Herbeck.

Hanslick, who was the sworn foe of Wagnerism and programme music, was interested in Dvořák's talent for absolute music. He was interested too in a talent which had formed itself upon the Viennese classical school, which was everything to Hanslick. He remained well disposed towards Dvořák, and gave his influential support to the young man's work, in spite of the fact that, although he himself was a native of Prague, he did not like the Czechs. Brahms, who also was not in sympathy with Wagner and the neo-German methods, valued both the quality and power of Dvořák's gifts, and recognized him as a great contemporary symphonist. It is certain that Brahms, with his deep and serious nature and his austere vein, admired Dvořák's genius, which revealed traits that Brahms consciously missed in himself. He appreciated Dvořák's naturalness, freshness and directness; his forceful temperament and simplicity of feeling—all features of a soul not overburdened with culture but saturated with racial characteristics. Brahms became Dvořák's generous and influential friend. Later on it was due to his intervention that Dvořák's works reached the outside world. He was Dvořák's adviser and, for a time at least, his leader. He influenced his music as regards its workmanship. Its sterling quality and perfect purity of outline and form owed something to him.

After Dvořák had won yet another prize, offered by the Umělecká Beseda (Society of Artists), with his String Quintet in G major—fresh and captivating, although not one of his deepest works —he returned once more, after an interval of three years, to lyrical composition. Again his choice fell upon folk-texts, which he found in Sušil's Collection of Moravian National Songs. This was the origin of the Moravian Duets, the first three of which appeared in March 1875. They were dedicated to Mme Neff, wife of the wholesale merchant of that name, who soon saw to their publication. Dvořák can hardly have foreseen that music so simple in form as these duets would open up the world to him. At any rate he passed on at once to other things. Three delightful examples of chamber music were all written at this time: the Serenade for Strings in E major (Op. 22), which afterwards became known abroad; the Pianoforte Trio in B flat (Op. 21), which, thanks to the springtide gladness and animation of its first and third movements, its capricious polka,

4

and the yearning tenderness of its slow movement, holds its own to-day against works of far more complex modern type ; the quiet, touching simplicity and refined charm of the Pianoforte Quartet in D (Op. 23) has only recently won the appreciation it deserved.

To his four existing symphonies another was now added which was destined to make a stir in the outside world. This Symphony in F (Op. 24), was composed in June and July 1875. It was not, of course, until much later that it won the admiration of Hans von Bülow, to whom Dvořák dedicated it in 1887, and by whom it was made known in Germany. Bülow wrote an unreservedly enthusiastic letter of thanks, in which he said : " A dedication from you who—next to Brahms—are the most God-inspired composer of the day, is a higher distinction than any kind of decoration bestowed by a prince. I accept this honour with the heartiest thanks."

The fact that one of the most distinctive of Dvořák's works waited four years for a performance can only be accounted for by the fact that concert enterprise in Bohemia was then in a poor way. The Symphony was produced at one of the Slavonic Concerts, at Žofin, by Adolf Čech, in 1879. It was published by Simrock a year after it had been dedicated to Bülow.

Meanwhile Dvořák responded once again to his hankering for the stage. Having won a definite success with his comic opera, *The Pig-headed Peasants*, he now desired success in the field of serious and tragic opera. *Alfred* he acknowledged as a failure and completely cast it aside. Šourek expresses the opinion that Dvořák, in his new work, *Vanda*, wished to create an heroic Slavonic opera, anticipating perhaps a work of the same type as Smetana's as yet unknown *Libuša*. The original Polish text, by Juliana Surzycka, was arranged by F. Zákrejs and V. Beneš-Šumavský. It was again an impossible libretto, having an unintelligible historical plot, highly fantastic and unpleasantly sentimental; the scenic plan was bad, and finally the diction and versification were —according to Šourek—almost ludicrous. And, after all, there was nothing Slavonic in the whole libretto. It speaks well for Dvořák's strong creative spirit that thematically he was able to invest this weak text with a certain amount of musical interest. He has put into his leading motives, and into some entire scenes, a breath of the Slavonic spirit.

The half-year's work which Dvořák devoted to *Vanda* was not spent in vain, since it taught him greater sureness of operatic methods and brought him some recognition, even though the opera was not repeated after the first performance, on 17th April 1876. Cranz, the Hamburg publisher, purchased the work, but did not publish it. Šourek considers that it would only be possible to revive it to-day if the libretto were entirely rewritten.

A shadow fell on the Dvořák household while he was engaged upon this work : his second daughter was taken ill and died just as the score of *Vanda* was being completed.

This shadow darkens the compositions which come nearest to this period. A kind of melancholy rests upon the calm and meditative Pianoforte

Trio in G minor (Op. 26), and on the work which succeeded it—the String Quartet in E major, published later as Op. 80, to the great confusion of the critics ! As Smetana consoled his grief for the loss of his daughter Bedřiska by his Pianoforte Trio in G minor, so Dvořák found solace for his own sorrow in his *Stabat Mater*, which originated between 19th February and 7th May of this year.

During this period he did not complete the entire work. Probably he had neither force nor concentration for the task. The sketches made at the time of his trouble were worked out and orchestrated later on. This composition, which Šourek justly considers to be the foundation of Czech oratorio, is dedicated to the Union of Musical Artists, and should have been performed by them in 1877. The production was delayed for three years. Afterwards, however, the *Stabat Mater* made its way through the world. In 1883 it reached England where, under the direction of Sir Joseph Barnby, it achieved such a success at a concert of the London Musical Society, at St. James's Hall, that it was decided to repeat it the following year, when the composer was invited to conduct it. March 10, 1884, was the date of Dvořák's first great triumph in England—a triumph destined to be followed up by many others. The work born of his sorrow brought him this glad victory.

After completing the masterly score of the *Stabat Mater*, Dvořák, contrary to his usual custom, did not immediately set to work again ; apparently he felt unequal to fixing his mind upon

another broadly conceived composition. He wrote
a few comparatively trifling things, and gladly
listened to Mme Neff's advice to continue the
Moravian Duets. Sušil's collection proffered a
wealth of other poems for setting. A second cycle
of Duets soon appeared, followed a few months
later by a third. Both collections were published
in the winter of 1876 (Op. 32), with the Neffs'
assistance. When, in 1877, Dvořák again applied
for a share of the State grant, he enclosed these
duets, his latest work, with his application.
Brahms, already interested in Dvořák, found in
these duets a confirmation of his opinion of the
composer, and became zealous in the propaganda
of his works abroad. He wrote to Simrock in
Berlin, warmly recommending the Moravian Duets,
with a direct proposition to publish them, and
other works by Dvořák, "who, so they say, has
in hand a great many Czech operas, symphonies,
quartets and piano pieces." At the same time he
offered himself as an intermediary between the un-
business-like Dvořák and Simrock. A year later,
the Moravian Duets came out and attracted the
German musical world to a name hitherto unknown there. Henceforward the composer's reputation increased with each new publication
which appeared under the aegis of Simrock. Thus
Dvořák found a firm vantage-ground for his Muse.
He remained loyal to Simrock up to the time of
his death, only a few of his works being published
by other firms.

At the same time he also found a new dwelling,
to which he moved from the Rybníčka in 1877.
The chief reason for his move was that the pianos

near at hand threatened his work and quietude. At 12 Žitná Street he was at peace, for the landlord arranged so that the master should not suffer from other people's music. When asked by the author of this book why he chose Žitná Street, with its northern aspect and rather inconvenient situation, Dvořák answered with a roguish, mysterious gesture : " True—but there are no pianos ! "

Otherwise it appears that he was not easily disturbed during his work. He had a cosy study in his house, arranged in a simple middle-class style, but it was more used as a parlour. The master's favourite place to work in was the kitchen, where, at a small deal table, he sketched out his symphonies amid the sounds of domestic occupations. It is strange, however, that just at this time he clung to the very instrument which he most dreaded to hear !

Not long before his removal he wrote one of his most important works, the Variations in A flat major (Op. 36), and attempted a Pianoforte Concerto (Op. 33). In the latter, creative power did not entirely leave him in the lurch, but the piano retaliated upon his unfriendly attitude to it with some degree of spite. The piano part of the Concerto is not at all happy. Karel Sladkovsky, to whom the work is dedicated, found that this rather cold symphony with pianoforte *obbligato* offered but few opportunities for virtuosity.

The first part of 1877 saw Dvořák at work upon an opera. Very probably he was spurred on by the example of Smetana, whose *Hubička* (*The Kiss*) had appeared for the first time in the preceding autumn with splendid success. Dvořák began looking round for a libretto at once national and humorous ; but unhappily he again set a book which a more fastidious composer would have rejected—Josef Otokar Vesely's *Šelma Sedlák* (*The Peasant a Rogue*). The opera was produced on 27th January 1878. The first night was accounted successful, and the work has since been given from time to time on the stage. It is always well received. Abroad, too, it awakened interest, and performances in Dresden, admirably conducted by Schuch, and later in Hamburg, were quite successful. In Vienna it was impossible to repeat it, partly on account of the original distribution of the parts among inferior singers, and also because of a national demonstration from a certain section of the public.

The year was fruitful in other ways and produced works which raised Dvořák's reputation and carried it a step farther abroad. In September the Symphonic Variations for Orchestra appeared. This work in its original form, as produced by L. Procházka, is nearly forgotten. Not until ten years later, when Dvořák himself conducted it at one of the Slavonic Concerts, did he realize its value. Then he did not hesitate to propose that Richter should look at the score. The renowned conductor showed an appreciation of Dvořák's music equal to that of Bülow. He wrote to Dvořák by return : " I gladly avail myself of this opportunity of coming into touch with a composer by the grace of God. In any case I had been thinking that before my London scheme was quite fixed I would ask if you had anything for me. Now, your Symphonic Variations have come as a brilliant addition to my programme." The Variations were actually produced in London at one of the Richter Concerts in May 1887. After the performance Richter wrote : " I cannot remember a novelty having such a great success at any concert I have conducted." When, in December of that year, Richter again conducted the work at the Vienna Philharmonic Society, Brahms wrote to Dvořák : " So far no composition has made its way here like your Variations." The last composition of the year 1877 was a token of gratitude to Brahms for his friendship and warm interest in Dvořák's work. This was the String Quartet in D minor, only finished in December. Its intimate style, tender and delicate workmanship, and its affinity to Schubert accorded with Brahms's taste.

Now follow the years in which Dvořák's Slavonic sentiment, which in the preceding period had shown itself to be his most individual quality, took complete possession, dominating almost exclusively his style of composition. If the years between 1873–1877 constituted the springtime of his art, flowering vigorously in many-coloured blossoms, now his summer was at hand—a time when warmth and sunshine irradiated all his work.

After the success of the Moravian Duets, Simrock invited Dvořák to send him works in a similar style, but instrumental. The composer, anxious to show gratitude to another German well-wisher— the musical critic, Luwig Ehlert—dedicated his Serenade in D minor (Op. 44), for wind instruments, to him. Then he set to work on Simrock's commission. Dvořák's enemies were quick to

point out that he was now writing " to order."
But did not Raphael and many another great
painter work " on commission " ? Did not Mozart,
Beethoven and Berlioz also write to order ? The
commission offered to him at this time resulted in
nothing worse than the first series of Slavonic
Dances, a cycle of sparkling pieces over which the
world rejoiced as a new revelation in music—
works which seem to us to-day a clear embodiment
of Dvořák's genius. After the Slavonic Dances,
but deeper and broader in form, and more highly
polished in workmanship, while equally steeped in
the racial atmosphere, came the three Slavonic
Rhapsodies in D, A flat major, and G minor
(Op. 45). Such was the outcome of Dvořák's
compliance to Simrock and his so-called paltering
with his artistic conscience.

Undeterred by hostile criticism, the composer
resolved to write a few more works to order, and,
marvellous to relate, each one is more attractive
than the last. Josef Srb-Debrnov, the friend of
Smetana and Dvořák, had a harmonium in his
rooms, and this suggested to the latter the idea of
a miniature suite " Maličkosti " (" Bagatelles ")
for two violins, 'cello and harmonium instead of
pianoforte. In conception and tonal beauty, as
well as in purity of style, these movements are
exquisite. All the quiet smiling radiance and joy of
home life is in these delightful little domestic pieces.

About this time Joachim began to show some
interest in Dvořák's music. At his Chamber-
music Concerts in Berlin he gave two of the
master's works in June 1879, both of which were
contemporary with the Slavonic Dances : the

String Sextet in A (Op. 48), and the fresh and striking Quartet in E flat major (Op. 51), which Dvořák had completed at the close of 1878—undoubtedly one of his most popular works. Later on, Dvořák's relations with the great violinist led him to compose a Violin Concerto. While staying at the castle of Sychrov, near Turnov, as the guest of the Prince de Rohan, Dvořák wrote this work, which was finished in May or June 1879 and dispatched to Joachim to look through and touch up the solo part. The Concerto was not definitely completed until 1882, when Joachim produced it for the first time at one of his own concerts. In Bohemia, its first interpreter was František Ondříček, who played it in 1883. To-day, both Karel Hoffmann and Kocian regard the Concerto as one of their finest repertory pieces.

There was a kind of periodic movement in the master's method of working, and after the composition of works on a large scale, he almost invariably relaxed and wrote lighter and smaller pieces of an intimate character.

It was during such a period of rest that some of his most popular music saw the light : the two albums of Valses for piano, which are still most frequently played in his arrangement for string quartet ; an album of Mazurkas, also for piano ; and finally another Chamber work in a wholly intimate style—the Sonata for Violin and Piano (Op. 57), which in its tender, transparent loveliness makes no pretence to external effect.

A great work which had been slowly maturing in Dvořák's mind was completed in the autumn of 1880. This was his Symphony (Op. 60) in D

(erroneously described by his publishers as his
first), dedicated to Hans Richter in recognition of
his services to the composer. In the following
year the Symphony was given at one of the Slavonic
Concerts, at Žofin, under the conductorship of
Adolf Čech. No sooner published, than it made its
way abroad to Leipzig, Rostock (where it was
conducted by Kretschmar [1]), Graz, Cologne (under
Ferdinand Hiller), Frankfurt, New York and
Boston. Finally it attracted even the more
reserved public of England.

Hardly had Dvořák drawn breath after the
strenuous effort involved in this symphony, when
he composed the Legends, a cycle of ten pieces for
pianoforte four-hands, mostly calm and serious
in character, and dedicated to Eduard Hanslick.

He next turned his attention to a sketch for a
new opera. From March to October 1881, and
from February to September in the following year,
Dvořák was at work on *Dimitrij*. The score of
this opera had a strange destiny. Dvořák, who
was inclined to listen to the opinion of the critics—
sometimes even to those who were by no means
inspired or infallible—now reproached himself for
the lack of dramatic interest in his earlier works.
and was induced to revise *Dimitrij* repeatedly.
He first remodelled it in the summer of 1883, and
again, very drastically, during his visit to New
York in 1884, and also at his country house at
Vysoká. Kovařovic alone seems clearly to have
understood that obedience to the voice of
criticism was disadvantageous to the work, and

---

[1] Editor of the well-known Concert Guides, and Professor of Music
in the University of Berlin.

that the original score, as produced for the first
time in Prague, on 8th October 1882, under
Moric Anger, was really happier than any
subsequently revised version. Therefore the
National Theatre adopted the first draft of
Dimitrij, with a few cuts and improvements in
the declamatory phrases. The very latest edition
of the pianoforte score, made for the Umělecká
Besedá by Karel Kovařovic, also adheres to the
original form.

The remainder of the year 1882, when he was not
absorbed in *Dimitrij*, Dvořák spent chiefly in
writing his String Quartet in C major (Op. 61). The
fact that this work was composed for the Hellmes-
berger Quartet in Vienna may account for its
close sympathy with Beethoven and the Viennese
classical school. On the other hand, the incidental
and melodramatic music to Samberk's play, *Josef
Kajetan Tyl*, which dates from this time, is
saturated with the national Czech feeling. These
two works—the first deep and serious, the second
extremely popular in Bohemia in its day—filled in
the pause between a fresh outburst of strenuous
activity.

Dvořák inaugurated 1883 by a lofty and distinctive example of chamber music ; broadly
planned and noble, but unusually stern : the Pianoforte Trio in F minor (Op. 65).[1] It was finished
in March, when he passed on to the Scherzo
Capriccioso for Orchestra (Op. 66), destined later

[1] Šourek says that Dvořák drew upon this Trio for the D minor
Symphony (Op. 70), or that at least both works were inspired by
the same kind of agitated, and wholly subjective, experiences, " only
in the symphony these emotions burn with greater force and
passion."

on to become a favourite repertory number with Hans Richter. This was followed very soon by the impressive Hussite (Husitská) Overture, incomparable in its brilliance and classical finish. This powerfully built work is based on themes which reincarnated for Dvořák the past of his native land—the Chorale St. Wenceslaus and the Hussite Hymn, " All ye who are warriors of God " (" Ktož jste Boží bojovnici "). The two themes are, of course, at variance,[1] but the Overture itself proves that this variance is purely literary, not musical. The first performance of the work took place on 13th November 1883, at the reopening of the National Theatre after its destruction by fire. It interested Hans von Bülow, who was particularly sensitive to its purity of style. In spite of some hostile feeling to the country of its birth, Bülow repeatedly introduced the Hussite Overture into his programmes.

In this work Dvořák clearly approaches to programme music, but only in the widest sense of the word, just as Beethoven and Mendelssohn approached it in their overtures ; or Schumann, who was given to label his musical moods by attaching programmatic titles to some of his compositions. After he had completed " Husitská," Dvořák went on to write a cycle of programme pieces for pianoforte four-hands. He undertook this work at Simrock's instigation. He found himself in the same situation as Schumann. The

[1] The Hymn (fifteenth century), said to have been composed by the Hussite commander, Žižka, in his camp at Tabor, was undoubtedly sung by the Hussite army as they went out to battle. The Kyrielle St. Wenceslaus (tenth century) was adopted by the Catholic soldiers as a war-song.—[Editor.]

cycle was begun in the autumn of 1883 and finished in January 1884—but no titles had occurred to him. Even before he started on the work he lamented that he had no titles for the pieces, and that Schumann had exhausted all suitable names for these kind of compositions. Mme Červinková-Riegerová consoled him, saying : " If you have the music in your mind, what do the titles matter ? " The music was forthcoming, and eventually the names too, for the pieces were published under the general title of *Ze Šumavy* (Op. 68) (*From the Bohemian Forest*), and were called individually : 1. " In the Spinning-Room " ; 2. " By the Black Lake " ; 3. " The Night of St. Philip and St. James " ; 4. " At the Meeting - Place " ; 5. " Calm " ; 6. " From a Stormy Time." All the numbers are characteristic and poetical. They fall into two groups, each of which contains a climax in a tempestuous *Allegro.*

In the early spring of 1884, the master relaxed his strenuous diligence and remained silent for a time. There was good reason for this. I have already mentioned that Dvořák was invited to conduct the second performance of his *Stabat Mater*, given at the Albert Hall on 10th March. At the beginning of March he set off for London. The performance on a large scale, before an audience numbering two thousand, turned out to be an overwhelming success for the Czech composer. And an equal success awaited him ten days later at St. James's Hall, where at a concert of the Royal Philharmonic Society his Overture " Husitská " and the Symphony in D Major were enthusiastically received. The Scherzo Capriccioso and one of

the Slavonic Rhapsodies were given at a third
concert—this time at the Crystal Palace—and
several musical evenings were arranged in his
honour by Mr. Littleton, of the firm of Novello, and
the pianist, Oscar Beringer.

On his return composition moved slowly.
Dvořák was distracted by public engagements.
His own country was at last fully aware of the
value of its representative composer, and covered
him with marks of respect, not always quite
opportune. Everywhere the public wanted to
hear his now famous *Stabat Mater*, conducted by
himself. Hardly had he completed the sketch of
a new choral work on Erben's ballad, *The Spectre's
Bride*, when he had to prepare for another journey
to England. He left home on 30th August 1884, in
company with the writer, Vaclav J. Novotný, the
author of an excellent analysis of Dvořák's works.

Worcester was celebrating the eight-hundredth
anniversary of the foundation of the cathedral,
and Dvořák was bidden to conduct his *Stabat
Mater* on 11th September. "One of the finest
works of our times, and one which in general has
no rival," wrote one critic. Another wrote, after
the evening of the miscellaneous concert and the
performance of the Symphony in D major: "Respect and admiration, which the audience could not
repress, found vent in an outburst of enthusiasm."

Only after this new triumph the composer found
an interval of quiet in which to continue his work
upon *The Spectre's Bride*.[1] The score was finished

---

[1] The literal translation of the Czech title is *The Wedding Shift*
(*i.e.* chemise), which doubtless did not commend itself to the mid-
Victorian translator.

in the new year, at the summer residence which the composer acquired at Vysoká, near Přibam.

The small estate of Vysoká had been purchased by Dvořák's brother-in-law, Count Kounic. This democratic man of title married Dvořák's sister, Josefa Čermáková, a well-known Czech actress. The composer had often stayed there on visits, and was very fond of the attractive woodland surroundings. On his return from England he bought from his brother-in-law a piece of land and the shepherd's hut which formerly stood on it. A little one-storied cottage was soon pulled down and a pleasant house and garden made there. From that time forward nothing could keep Dvořák in Prague after the middle of June. He must be in Vysoká. There he found once more his country life, which, although his art had drawn him away from it, was always dear to him. There he reared his pigeons, which were a source of amusement to him and gave him more pleasure than the choicest society.

Even before the production of *The Spectre's Bride*, Dvořák turned to a work which proved to be a great and important pendant to his deep and passionate pianoforte Trio in F minor (Op. 65). This was his Symphony in D minor (Op. 70), begun on 13th December 1884. The work appeared in print as his second symphony, written for the Philharmonic Society of London. No sooner was the score off his hands—it was finished on 17th March 1885—than Dvořák was called away to conduct the first performance of *The Spectre's Bride*, by the Pilsen choral society " Hlahol," on 28th March, preparatory to leaving once more for

England. He travelled by way of Leipzig, Cologne and Calais, and was accompanied on this occasion by Dr. J. Zubaty. At the concert in St. James's Hall on 22nd April, the scenes of enthusiasm which had characterized his previous visits to England were repeated. He conducted the first performance of his Symphony in D minor in a masterly style. At a concert in May, the German pianist, Franz Rummel, introduced Dvořák's Pianoforte Concerto (Op. 27) to the English public. Finally the appreciation shown to his *Hymnus*[1] clinched Dvořák's fame in England.

He had to take a hasty leave of England in order to be present at the first performance of *The Spectre's Bride* in Prague. It was given there twice in the course of that year by the Prague choral association " Hlahol," under the conductorship of Karel Knittl.

For the time being Dvořák did not take up any very important work. He had again received an invitation to England. On this occasion it was to conduct *The Spectre's Bride* at the Birmingham Festival, the remainder of the scheme being directed by Richter. The work had already been brought within the reach of the British public by the publication of the pianoforte score, with an English translation, by Novello & Co. The performance occupied the third evening of the Festival, 27th August 1885.

According to the reports of the English newspapers, as the story was unfolded and Dvořák's

[1] Novello & Co. had already published an English version under the title of *The Heirs of the White Mountain.*

5

music increasingly stirred the feelings of the
public, a tremor of agitation passed through the
great Hall. This impression grew with every
fresh number, until each one was greeted with loud
applause, culminating in a thrilling climax when
the work came to an end. One critic declared
The Spectre's Bride to be "one of the most original
and important compositions of its kind ever given
at a Birmingham Festival." "The year 1885 will
be accounted glorious," he continued, "because it
has brought forward such a masterpiece."

Since the days of Handel and Haydn no composer
—except perhaps Mendelssohn—had been so
acclaimed in England. No festival programme
was now considered complete which did not
include an important work by Dvořák. New
works from his pen were anxiously awaited. Thus
for one of the chief days of the Leeds Festival, an
oratorio on a large scale was commissioned from
him, *St. Ludmila*. As soon as the composer
returned from Birmingham he started upon this
new work, the libretto for which was by the Czech
poet, Vrchlicky. He threw himself impulsively
into the subject, which offered such scope and
wealth of detail, and from 15th September 1885 to
the end of May 1886, devoted many hours a day
to the work. When he had completed the score
of the oratorio he still had the summer before him,
during which, at Simrock's request, he added a
second series to his most popular work, the Slavonic
Dances. The later collection, Op. 72, are not
less powerful than the first; they are, on the whole,
stronger as regards contents, and more mature on
the technical side. They were written in the

month of July, at Vysoká, and, like their predecessors, were first composed as pianoforte duets. The instrumentation, carried out in November under pressure from Simrock immediately after his return from his fifth triumphant visit to England, surpassed the first series in brilliance.

Dvořák himself shall relate the story of the first performance of *St. Ludmila* at Leeds on 5th October 1886. Writing home to Bohemia, he says : " Well, to-day it went off gloriously ! The performance lasted from 12.30 p.m. to 3 p.m. All the same, no sign of weariness—not the very least. The interest kept going to the last note ! I am still in the greatest state of excitement, partly the result of the remarkable performance of the orchestra (120 players), chorus (350) and soloists of the first rank ; and also on account of a magnificent ovation on the part of the public. The enthusiasm—this English enthusiasm—was such as I have not experienced for a long while ! I confess that I have never before been so strongly moved, nor so sensible of the flutter of excitement around me at the conductor's desk as after the first and third sections. At the close of the performance I had to bow my thanks again and again in response to a tempest of applause and the calling of my name. Then I had to speak a few words of praise in English, heartily congratulating the orchestra and chorus. Again the audience broke into tempestuous applause, waved their handkerchiefs and shouted my name. I heard that at Ludmila's aria, ' O grant me in the dust to fall,' which the famous Albani sang divinely, the public was moved to tears."

The 24th of October 1886 found Dvořák back in Birmingham to conduct his Symphony in D minor; while on the 29th of the same month he directed *St. Ludmila* at St. James's Hall, and a week later *The Spectre's Bride* at the Crystal Palace. This cantata was also performed three days later at Nottingham, but the composer was unable to conduct it on account of an important concert in Prague. He relinquished the baton to Richter.

While the master's fame grew until it surpassed that of any other Czech musician, the end of the year slipped by. On his return to Vysoká, Dvořák wrote as a relaxation the Four Songs in the folk-style (Op. 73), two of which, "Good-Night" and "The Maiden's Lament," soon became household words outside Bohemia. At the beginning of 1887 he was still resting from serious labours, for the Terzetto for Two Violins and Viola (Op. 74) and the Romantic Piece for Violin and Piano (Op. 75) are works of an intimate, domestic kind which I consider among his less important compositions. To the same period and category belongs the Mass in D, for mixed voices and organ, afterwards arranged with orchestral accompaniment.

Was he perhaps gathering strength during this time for certain future works which mark a high tide in his creative activity?

It looks as though it were so; for his Pianoforte Quintet in A (originally Op. 77, but now known as Op. 81) was composed between 18th August and 8th October 1887, and is certainly the noblest pianoforte quintet in the world's literature of

chamber music. *Jakobin*, begun in November
and finished in December 1888, ranks probably as
the most effective Czech opera after those of
Smetana. And again, after a short breathing-
space, in which he wrote a few songs and the
popular cycle of piano pieces " Poetical Tone-
Pictures " (Op. 85) (3 books), came a work as fresh
and full-blooded as the Pianoforte Quintet—the
brilliant Pianoforte Quartet in E flat (Op. 87),
completed at Vysoká, 19th August 1889. The
lovely, idyllic Symphony in G (Op. 88), so light-
hearted in tone, followed immediately. The score
is headed by an inscription : " To the Bohemian
Academy of Emperor Franz Joseph for the En-
couragement of Art and Literature, in thanks for
my election." At this period Dvořák occasionally
broke away from his publisher Simrock, and this
work, frequently called " The English Symphony,"
was published in London by Novello.

After Dvořák's successes, the Committee of the
Birmingham Festival invited him to write a work
for 1891, and suggested a setting of parts of Cardinal
Newman's poem, " The Dream of Gerontius."
Dvořák declined the subject, but promised a work
for the occasion. This was his solemn *Requiem
Mass* for solo voices, chorus and orchestra (Op. 89),
which he sketched out between January and June
1890. In August and September he polished the
work and put the finishing touches to the score
in Prague. Then, once again, he turned to chamber
music and wrote, in a new and remarkably original
style, a work in an agitated and variable mood :
the " Dumky " Trio (Op. 90), completed in February
1891.

A new office now claimed his time and strength when the post of Professor of Composition at the Prague Conservatoire was offered to him. Dvořák accepted the position and evidently devoted himself with great energy to the unaccustomed work of teaching. As early as the following May he was able to congratulate himself upon the first-fruits of his labours when, at a composers' evening in the small hall of the Conservatoire, he conducted some of his pupils' essays in composition and a few foreign works orchestrated by members of his class. Among the names of those who afterwards distinguished themselves were Oskar Nedbal, Otto Berger of the Czech String Quartet, Vojtěch Madlo, Kuchynka and Julius Fučik.

His own creative work had practically to be laid aside at this time. Only in the summer holidays he found leisure to compose a great work again— the cycle of three overtures originally entitled " Nature, Life and Love." [1] They had been as it were anticipated in their programmatic tendency by the Overture " Husitská." The first of the cycle, " Amid Nature," is dedicated to the University of Cambridge which had bestowed upon him the degree of Doctor of Music, *honoris causa*, earlier in the year. For the same reason he dedicated the second Overture " Carneval " to the Prague University. The third of the cycle is the impassioned and rather sombre " Othello."

Between the composition of the " Carneval " and " Othello " overtures occurred another English visit.

[1] The overtures, in spite of a general title, " Nature, Life and Love," are published as separate opus numbers—91, 92, 93.

On 9th October 1891, Dvořák's *Requiem* was performed for the first time at the Birmingham Festival, under his own direction. Again he had a decisive success and a hearty ovation at the end of the concert. The critics, however, did not place the *Requiem* on a level with the *Stabat Mater* or *St. Ludmila*. But they spoke of it as a work which "carried one away," and praised the almost sensational realism of the terrors of the Judgment.

Dvořák's success in Germany, and more especially in England, had now carried his reputation still farther afield. America wished to acquire him for its leading musical institution, the New York Conservatoire. The master bound himself for two years for a salary which, according to Czech standards, amounted to something like wealth. He received leave of absence from Prague dating from November 1892.

Dvořák found the departure for a long sea voyage difficult and hard. It was hard, too, for all who were accustomed to look to him as the pride and glory of Czech national music. Every town in Bohemia wanted him for a farewell concert before he started on his journey. On this tour Ferdinand Lachner (violinist) and Hanuš Wihan ('cellist) accompanied the master, and the work most frequently played was his latest production, the "Dumky" Trio. The Rondo for 'Cello and Piano (Op. 94), a fine thing which Dvořák wrote at the time for Wihan, was not orchestrated until 22nd October 1893, in New York.

His first greeting to the New World—perhaps because it had to be prepared beforehand—was decidedly conventional. As early as June 1892, at Vysoká, Dvořák was engaged in composing a " Te Deum " (Op. 103) in honour of the Columbus celebrations, to take place in New York on 21st October, when the composer directed the first performance. The Festival cantata, *The American Flag* (Op. 102), words by Rodman Drake, was also sketched out at Vysoká and orchestrated in America.

The harvest of Dvořák's American visit is not rich numerically, because it consisted of works on a large scale, but it may be compared to a full harvest of the purest and heaviest corn, without chaff. New surroundings now added a special colour, a local colour, to his music, which, since it shows some link with the people—Indian, Negro or American—we have got into the habit of calling " American."

From January to 24th May 1893 he was busy working upon a symphony on which all his creative faculties were concentrated at this time : The Symphony, No. 5, in E minor (Op. 95), called "From the New World." The first performance took place by the New York Philharmonic Society, under Anton Seidl, on 16th December 1893. The Symphony was introduced to Prague by the composer himself at a concert in the National Theatre after the vacation of 1893.

Later on, as though he wished to express his impressions of America in all musical forms, he set to work on two important examples of chamber music. His summer residence in America was at Spillville (Iowa), and during the holidays, between June and August 1893, he was occupied with the

String Quartet in F (Op. 96), and the Quintet, with two violas, in E flat (Op. 97)—two works unequalled for their temperamental vigour and brilliance. Following immediately upon these came the customary series of more homely compositions : the Sonatina for Piano and Violin, slight in style and subject-matter, dedicated to his children ; the Pianoforte Suite in A, equally fresh and light, showing in the weaving of the ideas some touches of American local colour ; finally, the genial, humorous and in its simplicity Haydn-like Humoresque for Pianoforte (Op. 101). About this time, too, may have originated the Biblical Songs [1] (Op. 99)—that fervent and wholly intimate expression of Dvořák's deep piety. And in order that even the field of virtuoso music should not be entirely neglected, he began the Violoncello Concerto (Op. 104), in November 1894. It was finished in New York on 9th February 1895. The last movement had been revised early in June of the previous year at Vysoká. The concerto is dedicated to Wihan, who, however, never performed it. [2] It was first played in London, in March 1896, by Leo Stern, who also introduced it to Prague in the following April at a concert of the Philharmonic Society, under the conductorship of Kovařovic. Since that time it has kept its place in the repertory of all the leading 'cellists. Becker and Casals gladly return to it, and Ladislav Zelenka, of the Czech String Quartet, has given it a revived rendering which is as beautiful as it is lucid.

[1] They are actually dated March 1894.
[2] Wihan accepted the chief professorship of the violoncello in the newly organized Conservatoire in Prague, where he died in 1920.

America would gladly have kept Dvořák in thrall for the rest of his days. The Americans did not recognize him as the English had done, merely as a great and satisfactory composer of oratorios and symphonies equal to the demands of English taste. America saw him as something higher. Musically sterile, she had waited until this Czech gave her something of a national art, just as the German Handel had endowed unmusical England.[1] Therefore his works were received so enthusiastically there, especially those which were shot through with " American " rhythms. But in spite of the great appreciation shown to him across the Atlantic, Dvořák was drawn back to his home.

In March 1895 he had already written some part of a quartet in New York, but it was not finished. A month later he left America for good, arriving home on 27th April. Apparently his brain was teeming with ideas, for he put aside the half-completed quartet and wrote another one. The pair of works, finished towards the end of 1895, closed the master's list of chamber music. The Quartets in A flat and G (Opp. 105 and 106) were his last and highest achievements in this line.

Perhaps it was wisdom on Rossini's part to give up composing operas after *William Tell*, aware that he would never be able to surpass this master-piece. Perhaps, although for a different reason, Dvořák truly believed—and occasionally asserted—

[1] The writer has fallen into an unaccountable error. Handel had the advantage of a pause in our creative musical activity, and of a facile acceptance of his art, while we were under a Hanoverian dynasty. A country which could already point to the Tudor period, to a Byrd and a Purcell, offers no analogy with unmusical America in the last decade of the nineteenth century.—[Editor.]

that all had been put into the old framework of
the sonata-form that could be expressed in it;
that absolute music was exhausted, and without
a literary basis nothing new could be brought into
the conventional forms. At any rate, from the
beginning of 1896 he turned his attention exclusively to programme music and opera.

I learnt from his own lips the reason why he
valued opera so highly. It was, so he explained
to me, because this was the one form of music
which must live in the people; which the people—
ourselves as much as the Italians—can feel and
experience in themselves. Therefore he wished to
create an art in this democratic sense.

Searching for subject-matter for the Symphonic
Poems he contemplated writing, he found it in a
book which was very near and dear to him on
account of its full, yet simple, contents in the folk-
tale style, told in expressive language that kept
close to the vernacular. This was Erben's *A
Garland of National Legends*, from which he drew
programmes for his Symphonic Poems, " Vodník "
(" The Watersprite ") (Op. 107), " Polednice "
(" The Midday Witch ") (Op. 108), " Zlatý
Kolovrat " (" The Golden Spinning-Wheel ") (Op.
109), and " Holoubek " (" The Wild Dove ")
(Op. 110). Although these works were composed
in one continuous series, they are not intended
as a cycle. The sketch of " Vodník," begun on
6th January, was finished in four days. " Polednice," which followed immediately, was sketched
out in three days. " Zlatý Kolovrat " was started
half-way through January. But the instrumentation, which surpassed in brilliancy anything he had

done so far, was begun after 24th January, and in the case of any of these compositions did not take him more than a few days. "Holoubek" originated a little later, the sketch dating from June, and the finished score from 26th October to 18th November 1896.

The last of Dvořák's Symphonic Poems was composed at Vysoká in August and October 1897, probably without any previously prepared programme. Dvořák played the nameless work to his pupil, Vitězslav Novák, and asked him what he thought of it. Novák replied rather hesitatingly: "It seems to speak of something heroic." This idea appealed to Dvořák, and did to some extent indicate the meaning of the music. It was, therefore, named "A Hero's Song" (Op. 111).

The first performance of "Vodník" took place at the Prague Conservatoire under the direction of Knittl; the first public hearing—together with "Polednice" and "Zlatý Kolovrat"—was at one of the concerts of the Philharmonic Society, conducted by Adolf Čech, on 24th April 1897. In the course of the same year Janáček gave "Holoubek" at Brno. "A Hero's Song" was produced by Gustav Mahler in Vienna, 1898.

Having given musical expression to Czech legend, Dvořák returned to opera, employing the same kind of literary basis. He now set two fairy-tales to music. Between the spring of 1898 and February of the following year he was engaged upon *Čert a Káča* (*The Devil and Kate*), and no sooner had the work caught on with the public at the National Theatre than he became absorbed in the setting of Kvapil's *Rusalka*. He was so carried away by his enthusiasm for the subject that the whole score was completed between 19th May and 27th November 1900. The first night of this—the most popular of all Dvořák's operatic works—took place on 31st March 1901. It was conducted by Kovařovic, the newly appointed conductor-in-chief of the National Theatre.

With this setting of a lyrical legend Dvořák reached the zenith of his operatic work, just as he had touched the highest point in his purely instrumental music with the Symphony, " From the New World " and the Quartets (Opp. 105 and 106).

Alas, that the stage should have disappointed him in his last hopes ! It rarely happened that Dvořák passed the limitations of his creative powers, of which he was most scrupulously aware. Among his greater works there is only one of which this could be said, and it is painful to remember that it was his last. Evidently in his latest period he was ambitious of going beyond all that he had so far achieved. But in this case he did not surpass himself : he went astray. He was tempted out of his path by the romantic and fantastic elements of Vrchlicky's *Armida*. From early in April 1902 until August 1903 he was engaged in an unusually long struggle with material which cruelly defied him. But he was determined to conquer. He wished to give of his very best and to answer here once for all the hitherto unfulfilled claims of the dramatic style. It was to be his convincing reply to those who still reproached him for his shortcomings in this respect. But in this work the dark patches proved stronger than the high lights. *Armida,* first produced at the National Theatre on 26th March 1904, under the direction of Picka, fell flat. This failure, coming at the climax of his career, was a mortal blow to Dvořák. He who had never known what sickness was, fell ill in the month of April. It was thought to be influenza, but it was something worse. The end came unexpectedly, after—as so often happens—an appearance of improvement. He died suddenly at the dinner-table on 1st May.

On a lovely spring day (5th May), a long procession, in which many of his countrymen took part, followed his coffin to the churchyard of the Vyšehrad, and every year we remember on this anniversary to do honour to the musician who, after Smetana, remains nearest and dearest to the Czech people.

PART II
COMPOSITIONS

PART II.—COMPOSITIONS

IN order to characterize Dvořák's instrumental
works—that is to say, the published and
well-known compositions—it almost suffices
to divide them into two broad categories : Symphonic and Chamber music. In other instrumental
spheres he only worked incidentally and produced
music of minor importance.

Let us glance first at his pianoforte music.
Most of his compositions in this line originated at
the prompting of his publishers, and many of these
works show, side by side with touches of genius,
evidences of slight and hasty workmanship. Among
the compositions of deeper significance which, as
regards matter and firmness of structure, rest to
some extent upon the influence of Beethoven and
Brahms, I will mention only the Variations in
A flat major (Op. 36), which, as music, are certainly beautiful in their restraint, although perhaps
not altogether pianistic. With this may be grouped
the album of Poetic Moods (Op. 85), one of the
best things in our pianoforte literature. These are
valuable for the emotional variety they contain :
the tender, dreamy, half-suppressed voice heard
in the " Twilight Way " and " In the Old Castle " ;
the inspired melody of " Sorrowful Reverie " ; the
fascination and capricious humour of the charming,

6

old-world " Serenade " ; the force and temperament poured forth in the " Furiant " and " Peasant's
Ballad " ; the ringing sonority of the " Goblin's
Dance " ; the clever " Gossip " and the noble
pathos developed in the sorrowful scene, " At the
Graveside." The pieces are valuable also for their
wealth of ideas, and the long-spun thoughts are
here characteristic of Dvořák's manner in later
years—a manner generally favoured by him in
his works for pianoforte, not strictly organic but
rather cyclic. The pianistic style is original, the
colour mostly light and ethereal, now sparkling,
now carried on in broad lyrical sonority. The
" Humoreske " (Op. 101) is typical of the American-
ized Dvořák. The structure verges upon the
primitive in its simple, regular eight-bar rhythm ;
here he exploits the instrument as little as possible,
yet the piece sparkles with Dvořák's particular
capricious quips and turns and is clothed in the
most prismatic harmony.

Dvořák also composed several things for pianoforte four-hands in quite a different style, being
symphonic in conception, and now more frequently
heard in orchestral versions. Such are the two
series of Slavonic Dances, the Legends and the
cycle, " Z Šumavy " (" Aus dem Böhmerwalde ")
(Op. 68).

We have seen how the Slavonic Dances took the
world by storm, the more so that they appeared
at a time when it was yearning for new musical
manifestations and expected to find them in
racial art and in nations as yet unexhausted by
old culture. It was the moment when the national
style in art began to be highly appreciated—and

rightly so. Therefore the Slavonic Dances came
as a direct revelation. They are not imitative, or
manufactured by an exotic, but adaptable, musician.
They spring directly from the soul of the people.
Something of our Slavonic soul speaks in every
theme we meet in them. We find the stormy,
high-spirited mood characteristic of the first and
last sections of the Furiant in both examples of
this form given in the cycles ; there is whimsical
merriment, charm and a touch of coquetry, or
the contrast of ardent lyricism, in the ditties of
the peasant girls ; or, again, the slow, robust
rhythms of the minuets recall a bygone day. As
regards colour, the first series contains individual
numbers definitely Czech in style, whereas in the
second cycle the composer ranges farther afield.
Here the first number, in B major, and the *Presto*,
in C, are Yugoslav in character, while the second
number is a little Russian "Dumka."

In their special style the Slavonic Dances have
a power which carries us off our feet, to which
they owe their triumphant success, for such fire
and temperament were, and are, extremely rare
qualities in music.

The more precious, therefore, are all these
features, because they bear also the stamp of
classical clarity, purity and fastidiousness of
workmanship. The structure of the Dances is
delicate, the counterpoint characteristic, the figuration original and the orchestral colour masterly.
In every respect these Dances are symphonic in
technique, and take their place in the front rank
of the music of the nineteenth century.

The cycle, " Z Šumavy," is equally symphonic

in style, especially as regards fulness of invention.
The national tendency is less definitely in evidence ;
but the workmanship is equally finished and the
moods evoked by the forest scenes are graphically
characterized. I have particularly in mind the
number called "Waldesruhe," which, in its sub-
sequent arrangement for solo violoncello and
orchestra, is known as one of the loveliest and
most poetical of Dvořák's inspired *Adagios*.

We will now pass on to the very core of the
composer's art—to his chamber music and symphonies.

In chamber music Dvořák repeatedly returned
to the form of the string quartet, and these works
alone would suffice to create the image of his
personality, at least in its main features, so deeply
are they penetrated by the spirit of the man himself. I will restrict my observations to the published quartets which are accessible in the miniature
scores issued by Ernest Eulenburg of Leipzig.

Probably the first of these was the Quartet in
E major, published as Op. 80, but actually Op. 27.
This is a work of great delicacy, both of workmanship and feeling—chamber music in the most
restricted and classical sense. Here the composer
is so greatly influenced by Beethoven and Schubert
that many of his idiosyncrasies are not revealed at
all in this music. He has evidently restrained
the ebullition of temperament, repressed emotional
fire, and given out merely a hint of the national
style. I have already mentioned that at this
time Fate set a *sordino* upon the vehement and
seething power which was agitating him, and
damped his impetuosity. The Quartet reflects

his frame of mind after the loss of his little
daughter.

Very close to this Quartet in its delicacy of
style, is the one in D minor (Op. 34), dedicated to
Brahms. The mood, however, is brighter than in
the preceding work, the entire composition being
flooded by a lovely warm and tranquil light. It
is also dominated by the great tradition of the
Viennese masters ; there is less of Beethoven's
influence and more of the romantic tenderness and
mellifluent beauty of Schubert. The first movement echoes the fervent tone of this master, and
his sprightly and capricious quadrille-rhythms,
such as he uses in his finales, also prevail in the
last movement of Dvořák's Quartet. It is interesting to observe that here, in spite of a close affinity,
Dvořák never loses his identity. The relationship
is only spiritual. The Scherzo movement also
follows the style of this master ; here, however,
the folk-dance is not the valse, or Viennese Ländler
of Schubert, but a delightful slow polka, with an
equally charming trio in 3/8—a purely Czech
dance-form by a purely Czech Dvořák. Nor is he
less himself in the ballad-like *Adagio*, a long-
drawn emotional melody in which a touch of
Yugoslav colour is added to its Schubertian
warmth. Very charming in its way is the effect
produced by subduing the coda after its moment
of greatest tension by means of a tributary idea
recalled from the opening movement.

Another Quartet, in E flat (Op. 51), dates from
1879. It bears every mark of that happy time in
Dvořák's creative activity which we have pointed
out as his " Slavonic " period. Here, throughout

the work, there is no thought of outside influence. It is purely and only Dvořák who speaks. We have only to hear a few notes in order to define the race and country of the composer; the meditative melody of the leading movement, and its genial polka theme with its lively rhythm, which is made use of later on; the humorous second subject is treated contrapuntally in combination with another gay rhythmic figure—such simple material, but so characteristic, and built up with a masterly classical touch. Fresh rhythmic and tonal effects keep bubbling up, and yet they do not break through the perfect organism of the first movement.

The second movement is called a "Dumka" (G minor). The title gives us the cue to its contents. It falls into two sections. A broad, melancholy theme, Russian in character, is the basis of a dialogue between violin and viola which forms the principal portion of the movement. The second section, which alternates twice with the Dumka, is a gay and spirited *Vivace* in the major, being in the Czech dance-form of the Furiant. Because the Dumka winds up with this quick movement (although on its second repetition it is slightly overshadowed by the change to G minor) and the capricious fluctuations of its mood hinder the full expression of the lyrical element, the composer follows it by a short, slow movement, a Romance. It moves in broad, sustained lied-form, simply and quietly, until it is presently contrasted with an *Intermezzo* which stands between it and the finale. Here a purely Czech dance, the *skočna*, is treated in sonata-

form. There are two leading ideas : one high-
spirited and persistently recurrent, the other
whimsical and gay. The movement is carried on
with unrestrained and truly Dvořák-like humour.
The return to the recapitulation is beautiful, and
the coda, in which both the leading motives
frequently recur, captivates us by its tempestuous
gaiety.

For its striking originality, teeming variety of
subject-matter, and pleasant, sunny, laughing
atmosphere, as well as for its masterly technique,
I consider this to be an outstanding example not
only of Czech chamber music, but of this type of
work in general.

The Quartet in C major (Op. 61) offers in many
respects a complete contrast from the preceding
one. So far, Dvořák has led us through his native
land, all abloom with flowers on a bright, warm
day. Here he spreads his wings and soars in bold
flight up to the classic sun—to Beethoven's ideal
beauty. It seems as though he would shut
out all vision of his own land. No one has
ever drawn such direct force from Beethoven as
Dvořák does in this broadly planned and splendid
work. He rarely rises to such heights as here.
I think that something purely terrestrial, some
odour of earth and our Czech soil, is almost always
linked to the personality of our master. But this
quality, this fragrance, rise here to such celestial
heights as they could never have reached of themselves. In this work he has drawn so close to
Beethoven that the disciple has paid the price of
halving his soul with the master.

The Quartet in F (Op. 96) originated from

Dvořák's invitation to America, and, like the work discussed above, occupies a peculiar and isolated place, apart from the quartets inspired at home. If externally the Quartet in C major reveals the closest adherence to Beethoven's manner, and to his organic and polyphonically developed forms, the F major Quartet shows how far, on occasion, Dvořák could travel from the classical style and methods. The world on the other side of the Atlantic offered to his eyes and ears an entirely different aspect of music. Rhythm comes to the fore as the chief element. Note the thematic material. The usual style of Dvořák's rhythm now takes on a sort of brusqueness. The themes themselves now have a new colouring, and on the melodic side we observe the use of the æolian, or mixo-lydian seventh, the subdominant with the augmented sixth, and other peculiarities unusual in our music. The composition which he built upon these themes is far removed from that organic depth and elaborate polyphony which are so noticeable in Dvořák's preceding works. It seems as though he wanted to catch quickly, and set down simply, his first impression of the New World, with its Negro Melodies, its hustling life, its varied and vibrant colour. It is all there as our master saw it. These new types, this bustling movement, this novelty, this play of light and shade, were made evident to him. And he reacted to it all to the fullest extent. The Quartet cannot fail to interest us by its originality, and here we may use a term so exceptionally applicable to Dvořák—by the " exotic " charm of the ideas, rhythms and melodies. Nor can we fail to be dazzled by Dvořák's virtuosity in all that concerns colour and by the remarkable " go " of his rapid movements. It is one of those works so direct, so full of almost barbaric force, that we only recognize its negative qualities when we are away from its ravishing and spell-weaving charms. We cannot regard the peculiarly impressionistic style of the work as a fault.

Much the same may be said of a composition which originated about the same time as the American Quartet, the leading features of which approximate very closely to it. The String Quintet, with two violas, in E flat major (Op. 97), once more registers the first musical moods and impressions of Dvořák's American visit. Here a new ennobling element is introduced—the devout religious sentiment which pervades the slow movement (*Larghetto*). There is a link between this movement and the sublime lyricism of the Biblical Songs, which also took rise in Dvořák's heart about this time. Polyphony and organic form apart, the Quintet is a richer work than the Quartet, all the striking features of which reappear here in much stronger form. Its melodies and rhythms again bear the stamp of the Negro songs, and the rushing movement and unbridled temperament of the *Scherzo* show traces of the same source of inspiration. The wonderful finale is worked up to an orgy of sound and wild rhythms. Here is a power verging on brutality. Here, too, we have a magnificent sonority and beauty, although of a savage and barbaric order.

Beyond the impressions caught and fixed in these two works, Dvořák has told us nothing further about the American world in his chamber music. Once more he withdrew into himself. The last Quartets, in A and G major (Opp. 105 and 106), are revelations of a more settled condition of soul after having seen, experienced and created so much. With these works he took leave of America and hailed his own country, to which he now returned.

All the strongest and most beautiful qualities in Dvořák's nature are combined in these works : the poetry and freshness of youth, the virile strength belonging to his time of life, the depth and over-flowing tenderness, the harmonious sweetness of approaching old age. All that pertains to foreign lands is superfluous here. We find the climax of sunny gladness and glowing happiness which belongs to his own home. Once more we are back in our own Bohemia.

And in this music we find also all that the art of Dvořák had acquired in course of time. The composer now returns to the earlier examples of his work, to organic structural development and polyphony. The form is rich, the structure simple and concise. But it is significant that the wealth of colour dating from the period of his American visit is not displayed here as a predominant element, as mere sonority in itself, but as something organic which flows out of the whole plan of the work. There could be no more beautiful farewell to the quartet form !

I have already said something about Dvořák's chamber music associated with the pianoforte. His pianoforte trios, for instance : one in B flat (Op. 21), luminous, filled with the breath of spring

and the perfume of romance; another in G minor
(Op. 26), a dreamy, melancholy work in which
Dvořák already speaks in his own words, while
Beethoven guides the creator's hand; a third in
F minor (Op. 65)—sombre, overshadowed with dark
clouds, pregnant with combative energy, defiant,
muffled in tone, and showing in structure something of the influence of Brahms. If this work,
nobly conceived and worked out with rich instrumentation, is a great favourite with pianists
abroad, to the Czechs at home the most precious
of Dvořák's compositions in this style is his last—
the Dumky Trio (Op. 90).

Profound grief and sparkling gladness; melancholy monotony and earnest prayer; the silvery,
bell-like rhythm of the dance; the moonlight over-
spreading the broad plain, and dreamy, drowsy
moods by the banks of rushing streams; a wild
drunken orgy among the village lads; the slow,
stumbling footsteps of a dark funeral procession
crossing the hills; the whirlwind flight of red
elemental joy—the Dumky Trio speaks to us in
these contrasts. Only a composer of genius could
have invented this antithesis of moods, and only
an inspired stylist could have power to weld these
musical forms firmly and compactly into a whole.

The Trio is so full of shifting and fanciful ideas,
its form of six movements, alternating in slow and
lively *tempi*, is so entirely original, and the whole
is steeped in such poetic colouring, that the work
is undoubtedly one of the most remarkable examples
of modern chamber music. Although permeated
with the most intimate Czech sentiment, the
Dumky Trio was immediately welcomed abroad,

together with two other compositions which followed it—the Pianoforte Quintet in A major (Op. 81) and the Pianoforte Quartet in E flat (Op. 87).

The Quintet is one of Dvořák's most popular works, attuned as it is to one bright, and frequently glowing, tonality. A rich stream of melody flows through the first movement, reflecting sunshine and gladness. The Dumka, in rondo-form, is in quiet contrast and seems to sing of the darkened hills and the hope of dawn. In the place of an *Adagio* there is a characteristic Slavonic Dumka, and for a *Scherzo* Dvořák has substituted the accustomed Czech Furiant, overflowing with high spirits and animation. The *Finale* is charming, its humorous garrulity develops into a madcap, joyous, whirling dance, and makes a splendid wind-up to a brilliant work.

In the brightness of its mood the temperamental Pianoforte Quartet in E flat major stands in close proximity to the Quintet. Here the ideas are more in opposition to each other—masculine energy opposed to masculine tenderness. Emotional balance is the keynote of the work, in which there is no dark shadow of grief nor the slightest hint of excessive sentimentality. The invention and workmanship belong entirely to Dvořák, and owe nothing to his predecessors. Only in the Quintet there is an occasional link with Schubert. This music is already Dvořák in his latest period, when he preferred to think out his thematic material concisely and set his motives directly side by side in simple co-ordination. It is certainly the Dvořák of the period when he had attained to such luminous colouring in the grouping and laying on of his tints as makes this Quartet—in a different way—even more dazzling than the delicate " Dumky."

After the chamber music, the second most individual group of Dvořák's works are his symphonic compositions. Although his symphonies come first, the term may be applied to the whole of his orchestral music, for he was a born symphonist, and wrote very little for orchestra that was not symphonic in character.

After Dvořák's death, the firm of Simrock published two Symphonies : one in E flat major (1873) and the other in D minor. These works are both rich in ideas, finished as regards workmanship, and perhaps all the more attractive because of certain deviations from strict sonata form. The first is permeated by the romantic spirit which possessed Dvořák at this time. The second, which reveals extreme agitation of mood, is simpler in structure and employs a more modest orchestra. It is based rather upon Beethoven than the neo-romantic school, but shows at times features which are quite personal to Dvořák.

But the real sum and substance of Dvořák's orchestral music consists in those five symphonies which were published during his life, in which he proves his maturity and shows that he has cut his way through to complete independence and individuality.

In view of the erroneous chronological arrangement of Dvořák's symphonies, I must point out that the earliest of these five works is actually No. 3, in F. (Op. 76). After it came the one in D

major (Op. 60), and still later the D minor Symphony (Op. 70), wrongly described as No. 2.
Kretschmar, in his analysis of the Symphony in
F (No. 3), justly observes that it is " pastoral." It
speaks of youth, of the ideal, of love, of conflicts
endured and of purgings of soul.

The scene of the first movement seems to be
cast amid nature and the rustling of trees—not
the deep, mysterious and haunting voices of the
forest, but the sweet murmurs of the woodland
clearings where the sun breaks through on a glad,
fresh day, and the breeze carries with it a distant
echo of the songs of the soil. Both the chief
themes on which the opening movement is built are
descriptive of its style.

and

The slow movement, in 3/8 measure, elaborates
two more important motives in a darker mood.
The *Intermezzo* is like an oppressive dream. But
the delicious valse-theme atones for it. And
further on comes an idyllic motive to which we
have been introduced in the first movement.
Dvořák wakes from this happy mood in the Finale.

This opens with the hot-blooded defiance of youth :

This energetic motive is carried on in a broad development. The second subject, which accentuates the tender, emotional aspect of the Symphony, scarcely makes itself heard through the rapid murmuring figuration of accompaniment.

In the rush of the accompaniment the energetic leading theme re-enters unobtrusively, and goes its way in a variety of light and shade. The joyous forces of life are now developed, flowing on in ever-increasing power. After this tumult the idyllic phase of the opening movement is recalled. The work ends with a brilliant fanfare.

After the Symphony in F came the so-called first Symphony in D (Op. 60), a work remarkable for its cheerful tone. The first bright and joyful theme announces that here the composer has no tale of great conflicts, catastrophes or heroic triumphs to unfold. Once again the first movement speaks of joy in nature, of idyllic happiness and simple emotions. An *Adagio* which is tender, dreamy, profound, but also quite simple and sincere, free from the least suspicion of neuroticism or gleam of passion, grows out of a broad lyrical

folk-song. For the *Scherzo* Dvořák employs a
Furiant, strong in its frenzied rhythms; full of
robust and potent vitality.

The last movement may best be characterized
by quoting its two leading themes :

Both subjects are overflowing with capricious
humour, and the second is finely worked out.

The Symphony in D minor (Op. 70) (called No. 2)
is exceptional among Dvořák's works because of
its deep shadows. Here, the dark mood which
smouldered through the nineteenth century is not
without its fleeting influence on Dvořák, who
was generally accessible to outside impressions.
Nor was the influence of his friend and counsellor,
Brahms, without practical results. This shows itself
here not only in the mental attitude but to some
extent in the invention, in which Dvořák, denying
himself, conforms to Brahms's lines and attains, as
far as technique is concerned, to a work of superb
and powerful scope which rises above its gloom in
perfect compactness and loftiness of spirit. It is
a beautiful, really grand, plastic work, like the
statue of some hero, his tragic and sublime gesture
half hidden by a dark drapery ; but neither the
image nor the gesture appear to us to represent
Dvořák. The same thing applies to the Quartet

in C major. Both works show the master at his
loftiest, and yet most remote from his truest and
most characteristic self. It is hardly possible to
analyse this work here, for an account of its rich
and complex structure would be beyond the scope
of this book.[1]

A complete contrast to the work we have been
discussing is the Symphony No. 4 (Op. 88), once
again in a bright, idyllic key—G major. It is
simple, straightforward music without any pretence
to scholasticism. There is no very deep problem
worked out as in the preceding symphony ; humour
and its fleeting devices prevail here. The work
as a whole seems to rejoice freely in its existence,
and its thoughts break into flower—not like little
blossoms lodged in the stony crevices of an archi-
tectural structure, but as the Czech meadows
flower, in luxuriant garlands of varied charm and
colour—a very unusual symphonic style. Here, all
is simplicity, even in the first movement, which is
planned in a delicious idyllic mood and only lets
itself go to some extent in its second march-like
theme. The lovely slow movement (*Adagio*) is
equally simple, in which a quiet, religious melody
is placed side by side with a series of coquettish
passages which are not in keeping as a slender accompaniment to a broad melody, like a serenade ;
eventually both motives are joined by the curt
and lively march rhythm.

Even the challenging trumpet fanfare which,
after a broad melodious *Allegretto*, announces the
entrance of the last movement, does not introduce

---

[1] The score bears the inscription : "Composed for the Philharmonic Society of London."

7

us to a strange new world. It is answered by a
theme formed from the chief subject of the first
movement, which runs

while the theme of the Finale is :

The variations which grow out of this theme have
the merry, boisterous character of a rustic festivity.

This Symphony is not profound ; it awakens no
echo of conflict or passion ; it is a simple lyric,
singing of the beauty of our country for the heart's
consolation; it is a lovable expression of a genius who
can rejoice with the idyllicism of his own forbears.

Dvořák's fifth Symphony, in E minor (Op. 95),
is called "From the New World." A series of
motives used as the basis of the work are connected
with America. This thematic material, like that
of the American Quartet and Quintet, has been
derived or imitated from Negro and Indian sources :

The characteristic rhythms of these tunes, and
some of their melodic peculiarities, are stamped
upon the entire work. But it is certain that, in
spite of this, the composer's connection with his
native land is far more intimate here than in either
of the chamber-music works in which he was
entirely preoccupied with his American impressions;
how close the tie is becomes evident as the note of
the "New World" intermingles more and more
with reminiscences of home. With the elemental
force of the first movement, the noisy, almost
barbaric, *Scherzo*, the combative mood of the
Finale, mingles a touch of lyric tenderness, and this
music—with the exception of the beautiful Indian
subsidiary melody in the first movement—often

seems to be steeped in thoughts of home. How exquisite is the lovely half-religious *Adagio*, with its melody for *cor anglais*—a feeling which could only have grown up in the vicinity of the Biblical Songs. And again in the second subject of the *Finale* he sings to himself a reminiscence of Bohemia which sounds completely as though it belonged to the fourth Symphony.

Of all Dvořák's works the "New World" symphony is the one which, in spite of its high standard of perfect artistry, leaves the impression of sheer simplicity. It is obvious how the various sections fall into line, and how easily they are evolved one from another. Because at this time Dvořák was more disposed to homophonic methods, the contrapuntal treatment is less predominant than in former works. But, as in the chamber music of this period, the splendid sonority of the Symphony is dazzling in effect. The fifth Symphony depicts Dvořák's restless life and all the varied impressions of the New World; but it speaks to us also in new expressive terms, in strongly accentuated rhythms and simple, clear-cut forms, of his longings for home. The whole idea is full-toned and gorgeous in colour.

[It is unnecessary to rake up the controversies provoked by Dvořák's natural interest in the tunes of the American Indians and the African negroes which were brought to his notice during his visit to the New World. Whatever melodic fragments he may have seen fit to use in his fifth Symphony, to those who are familiar with the folk-music of the Central European Slavs this work will always seem, in melodic material and rhythmic treatment, more akin to the Slavonic than to the Afro-American world. When I say " Slavonic " I entirely exclude that barbaric Muscovite splendour —Oriental rather than Slav—of which there is not a trace in Dvořák's music. But at the time of writing I have before me an interesting unpublished letter by the late E. H. Krehbiel, kindly put at my disposition by Mr. H. C. Colles, to whom it is addressed. The distinguished American critic saw a good deal of Dvořák at the time he was composing the Symphony " From the New World," and his observations show a balanced attitude to this once vexed question : Was Dvořák trying to create an " American music " out of these negroid folk elements ?

" *9th July* 1916.

" I shall answer your letter as fully as possible, for I am extremely desirous that Dr. Dvořák's attitude towards the Slave music of America shall be authoritatively set forth. I have pursued the misstatements concerning the 'New World Symphony ' here (in America) and abroad ever since the work was published ; but in this case, as in so many other cases, the truth cannot overtake a lie.

On some points I can venture information now :
There is no instance outside that which you mention
in which Negro themes are quoted in Dr. Dvořák's
music. I fancy that a fragment of ' Swing low,
sweet Chariot ' was consciously, or unconsciously,
quoted in the first movement of the ' New World '
symphony, but there is no draft upon Afro-American
folk-song in any other work. Two works quite as
much in the spirit of that folk-song are the string
quartet and quintet which followed the symphony,
but their themes are original. You will recognize
the rhythmical idiom and the spirit.

" That Dvořák was deeply interested in the
songs of the black slaves of America I know from
repeated conversations with him. I loaned him
some of my manuscripts, and he let me see the
symphony, quartet and quintet before they were
performed. He even went so far as to make a
pianoforte arrangement of the symphony which I
wanted for lecture purposes before the score had
been printed. I recall an amusing incident at the
interview which followed my bringing back to
him the manuscript. In the last movement there
is, you will remember, a recapitulation of the
themes of the preceding three movements. Ac-
companying the *Largo* melody there is a counterpoint started by the violas which is curiously like
' Yankee Doodle.' I laughingly called his attention to the resemblance and asked him if it was
intentional. He did not say no, but, ' Why, that's
the principal theme in diminution.' ' So it is,' I
replied, ' but isn't the principal theme " Yankee
Doodle " in augmentation and the minor mode ? '
He made no answer."

" He made no answer. . . ." Probably he did
not fully grasp the meaning of the question. The
incident reminds one of Tchaikovsky's reply in the
affirmative to a critic who asked him if he had not
used a Polish folk-song in the slow movement of
his third Symphony. Limited linguistic capacities
are answerable for much. That Dvořák's English
was far from fluent, Krehbiel proves in the con-
tinuation of his letter :

" Dvořák spoke English with his American and
English friends when he could not speak Bohemian
(Czech). He would answer a German question in
English unless his vocabulary was inadequate.
That was because of his Czechish patriotism."

These details seem to me of sufficient interest to
excuse my digression. Editor's addition.]

The development of Dvořák's symphonic music,
its unity of line and its steady ascent is completely characteristic of the rest of his orchestral
work, which is often not inferior in value to the
symphonies, and, no matter what its form, is
always symphonic in style. That is to say, that
every one of his orchestral works—the Symphonic
Variations, Rhapsodies or Overtures—springs from
a definite intelligible idea, and is presented in a
perfectly logical form which is the outcome of the
idea, unmixed with any fortuitous elements.

More particularly the two concertos for violin
and for violoncello deserve to be ranked beside
the master's symphonies for their skilful workmanship and admirable style. Since Beethoven's
time—with the exception perhaps of Brahms—no
composer had written a violin concerto which so
successfully solved the combination of the concerto

and symphonic styles as Dvořák's Op. 53, certainly
none which achieved so perfectly the elaboration
of such characteristic ideas in a distinguished
style, and fully satisfied both the demands of
virtuosity and the standards of good music. The
Concerto for Violoncello, although it perhaps
belongs to the period when his ideas were rather
co-ordinated than developed, remains one of the
finest works in the whole literature of the 'cello,
if not by its intellectual side, at least by its rhythmic
qualities, its intoxicating melodies, so well adapted
to the character of the solo instrument, and its
richly coloured, symphonic scoring.

So far, in reviewing Dvořák's works, I have barely
indicated that the composer revealed a tendency
to programme music in his Overture "Husitská"
and the early cycle "Nature, Love, and Life," and
that from the titles of his Overtures we may gain
some clue to their contents and the frame of mind
they depict.

On his return from America he entered more
thoroughly into the domain of the symphonic
poem, choosing as literary material the national
ballads of Erben. At first these methods of
composing were unaccustomed. We find him
adhering as closely as possible to the literary
basis. Not content to grasp its main features, he
tries to follow it step by step, section by section,
feeling for the musical equivalent. It is as though
he wanted to compose stanza by stanza, drawing
the themes actually from the rhythm of Erben's
verse. Such excessively detailed poems, apart
from the predominance of the epic over the
lyrical substance, and of the descriptive over the

emotional elements, do not seem most suitable
for symphonic poems, which should touch our
feelings, and can scarcely do so by means of pictorial
music. This type of very detailed ballad influenced Dvořák's work. His symphonic poems suffer
somewhat from the fragmentary nature of their
development. The musical composition is broken
up into a series of short sections; although, of
course, Dvořák's idea is finally revealed, thanks to
his rich and powerful gift of expression.

Moreover, these compositions suffer at times
from an exclusively pictorial style. The depicting
of purely external occurrences is, when all is said
and done, something foreign to music. Erben's
poems often demand excessive illustration, and
Dvořák, in his devotion to the poets whom he
drew upon, did not limit himself, like many other
musicians, to the mere indication of their moods.
But he often illustrated his programme with
wonderful truth and beauty, so that we are ready
to pardon his erroneous views on the subject of
the symphonic poem. It cannot be said that his
tone poems are firmly constructed, but as musical
conceptions they are rich and, when the literary
basis permits, or demands it, full of vivacity,
temperament and dramatic power. Above all,
his musical pictures excel as regards colour, and
for these reasons alone his latest symphonic works
are no unfitting climax to his life-work.

Side by side with Dvořák's chamber works and
symphonic music stand his vocal and vocal-
instrumental compositions. They are, as I have
already shown, greatly valued and appreciated
abroad. At home they have not won such general

recognition. Our critics once for all decided to place Dvořák in the category of the " absolute " musicians, which led to a certain failure in their appreciation of his vocal and choral works. Contemporary writers were hardly prepared to recognize him. They measured him by the only standard which was valid for them : Wagnerian declamation. No other measure existed for them. To this Teutonic foot-rule Dvořák could not be made to conform. Therefore he was inaccurately measured. But to-day the undervalued portion of his work lives as intensely as the portion which was first recognized. We sing his songs, perform his oratorios, his operas fill our theatres ; the same Czechoslavonic spirit breathes in them, the same wealth of individuality, and they are worked out with the same classical finish as the purely instrumental music. It is, moreover, significant of Dvořák's delicate sensibility that he never touched poetry which was in conflict with his temperament. His vocal music was composed only to words which awakened his emotions, and in which he found a sincere, and therefore convincing, musical note.

We have seen how he first displayed his youthful " Weltschmerz " in the song-cycle, " The Cypress Trees." He did not feel the excessive sentimentality of Pfleger's words — a sentimentality which in no way rendered them musically inferior. On the contrary he steeped this rather weak verse in his own young and vigorous ardour. His music, his luxuriant melody, gave external life to the colourless text.

Later on, when Dvořák had found his essential

Czech spirit, his songs at their best became direct
idealizations of the folk-songs.   The climax of his
lyrical music—the Moravian Duets—forms a vocal
analogy with the Slavonic Dances.   Every tone
and turn of the folk-songs is caught in these duets.
With the most modest means the composer has
succeeded in creating one of the purest and tenderest
works of what might be described as vocal chamber
music.   Next to them we may place the Songs in
the National Style, and third in order the cycle of
Gipsy Songs.   To the lyrical diary which enshrined
his youthful love dreams (" The Cypress Trees ")
and to the songs which expressed the patriotic
enthusiasm of his manhood, we must add the
missal-book of his advancing years—the Biblical
Songs, dating from his American days.   In this
cycle the simple, clear-cut words sing themselves,
firmly, unpretentiously, expressively.   They pro-
ceed from the voice of that deep faith and piety
peculiar to Dvořák among all modern composers
—with the possible exception of Bruckner.   Here
lyrical passages alternate with simple declamation.
The accompaniments are sketched in lightly, and
now and then the harmony discreetly illustrates
the meaning of the songs.   What an old-world,
truly Biblical impression they leave upon us !

Dvořák's love of folk-poetry and his religious
feeling determined the nature of his cantatas and
oratorios as well as the character of his songs.
We shall see, too, that in opera he tends in his
loftiest work towards nationality and the poetry
of the people.

Of all forms of popular poetry the epic appealed
most to his simple mind ; in adopting the artistic

formula of Erben's ballads we have seen the same tendency at work in his instrumental music. From Erben, too, he drew the poetic basis of the best of his secular cantatas, *The Spectre's Bride.*

For the purpose of musical setting Dvořák divided the poem into three main sections, linked to the three chief episodes of the tale : the scene in the maiden's little room, her night ride with the dead lover, and the scene in the churchyard. These sections are subdivided in accordance with the demands of the text into a series of solo numbers —the soloists are the maiden (soprano) and the dead man (tenor). The descriptive and narrative portions are given to the chorus. Occasionally the solo voices and chorus are heard in combination. The breaking up of a poem into such fragments was permissible in those days, but in forty years our views on the subject have entirely altered. Besides, Dvořák decidedly saved the poem by his music. He subordinated the claims of logical cohesion and flowing development. His music depicts the emotional phases of the individual scenes and dialogues with suggestive force. And Dvořák's innate tendency towards all that is lovely and bright saves him from monotony. Whenever it is at all possible he breaks through the fundamentally gloomy ballad tone with a ray of light. Again, there are parts of the work when the entire musical resources, vocal and orchestral, are employed to emphasize the sinister situations in the poem. The work, strong on the lyrical and emotional side, is not less interesting on the pictorial side, and contains some admirably graphic

incidents. As regards declamation, the reproaches
Dvořák incurred are actually justified. But we
must again remember that the art of Czech
musical declamation was not fully evolved at
that period. Even Smetana had not entirely
solved the question.

The noblest manifestation of Dvořák's religious
inspiration is his *Stabat Mater*. The mediæval
Latin sequence of Jacopone da Todi aimed at the
expression of his ideas rather than an attempt to
fathom the profound agitation and suffering of the
Holy Mother kneeling at the foot of the Cross. It
was Dvořák who decided upon the emotional content of his work. He did not regard the details of
the verse. Therefore he cannot be reproached for
having divided the text into a series of individual
numbers : choruses, solos and ensembles. The
words were divided in order to gain contrast and
plastic form. The broad and powerful development of the solo quartet and chorus extends
throughout the opening number like a grand
gesture : like the line of a vast range of hills. In
the eight numbers which make up the middle
portion of the work, lamentation (No. 2, " Quis
est homo ") alternates with supplication; grief
and solemn thoughts with outbursts, now passionate, now pathetic (No. 3, " Eia, mater " ; No. 4,
" Fac ut ardeat cor meum " ; No. 5, " Tui nati
vulnerate ") ; prayers full of sweet hope that
the suppliant may behold the glories of Paradise
(" Quando corpus morietur "). At the close of
the chorus (No. 10) another noble climax is built
up, rising to heights of supernatural light and
mystical rapture. The note of pain so frequently

heard in the introduction recurs again here, but only to remind us that it is overcome.

No oratorio dating from the second half of the nineteenth century has a greater wealth of ideas, artistically treated, or more fervent religious feeling, than Dvořák's *Stabat Mater*. The feeling which it expresses is purely Slavonic ; devout tenderness, humility and submission are all blended in this revelation of suffering. This is the Slavonic Mother of God whom the Slavonic musician invokes by his art.

To do honour to one of the national hero-saints had long been one of Dvořák's cherished wishes. He had in mind two such figures : John Hus and St. Wenceslaus (Vaclav). Jaroslav Vrchlicky's libretto of *St. Ludmila* finally attracted him away from these popular heroes of Czech history. Vrchlicky's text did not show any profound religious feeling—for that Dvořák had to rely entirely on himself. But the poet told the story of the conversion of Bohemia to Christianity in a series of noble scenes. In the first section of the poem there is plenty of contrast and dramatic movement ; the scenes of the middle portion offer more scope for lyrical music ; while the closing section deals with the triumph of the Christian faith. That the distinguished Czech writer relates these events in expressive and picturesque words none will deny. Upon this poetic basis Dvořák built up a musical triptych of colossal proportions, employing all his resources of intellect, skilled workmanship and instrumental colour to create an impressive—though perhaps too decorative— master-work.

The chief protagonists express themselves in a lofty tone, the accompaniments being equally epic in character, serene and elevated as befits the true oratorio style. Sometimes their language is sweet and winning, as in the case of Ludmila, sometimes impassioned and heartfelt, as in the utterances of Bořivoj ; or full of pathos and energy as when Ivan proclaims the new faith. The choral portions form a powerful background for the solos. Here Dvořák puts forth his full strength as though trying to surpass all previous efforts. How richly and nobly his well-chosen themes lend themselves to the complex fugal form. The choruses of Part I. are admirably suited to the pagan festival at the castle of Mělnik, and also to the following scene in which Ivan overthrows the statue of the goddess Bába, ending with the fine fugue, " Now all gives way together." But the crowning choral achievement is the closing number of the work, " Mighty Lord, to us be gracious," which rolls on sonorously in dazzling joyousness, with the whirling movement of a fanatical religious procession or dance. If the Biblical Songs are like a whispered prayer, if the *Stabat Mater* is like low Mass quietly celebrated in the heart of the composer—most surely we may liken *St. Ludmila* to a festival Mass chanted in some spacious cathedral by priests in rich vestments, amid clouds of incense and pealing of bells, and all the external pomp which took rise in the simple heart of Dvořák from his conception of solemn ritual.

Desiring to present scenes of such solemnity and brilliance, and to express such deep and fervent devotion, Dvořák, in this work, turned his steps

back to the traditional oratorio style of the past.
I do not think, however, that there is more justice
in accusing him of imitating Handel in *St. Ludmila*
than there is in the reproach that he copied
Beethoven in his quartet-writing. If the external
structure is sometimes Handelian, the spirit of
the work is wholly his own. It is the soul of
Dvořák expressing itself here : clear, tender,
joyous, without a shadow of austerity, and essentially Slavonic, *St. Ludmila* is not merely the greatest
Czech oratorio ; in style and feeling, in its sympathy with all human nature, it is a monumental
work of its kind.

There is yet one more important and highly
subjective religious work belonging to the composer's final creative period. Oppressive and
gloomy thoughts of " the last things " weighed
upon Dvořák with advancing years and found
utterance in his *Requiem.* He was not entirely
attracted by the dramatic features peculiar to
the Roman Mass for the dead. The terrors of the
Last Judgment repelled him. But that was only
one powerful and harrowing episode in the long,
sorrowful meditation and devout supplication
which made up the work. One motive which
extends throughout may be called " the re-
membrance of death " :

It constantly recurs and is used not so much as
an expressive theme as a deeply emotional link,
bringing both harmony and colour into closer

unity. It is a sigh of resignation breathed by a gentle Christian spirit which already feels a faint wind from the black pinions of the angel Asrael.

We have seen that all through his career Dvořák was attracted to opera. He constantly returned to this sphere of work in spite of the fact that he often met with disappointment and that probably his work for the stage brought him more bitterness than any other branch of his calling. Some operas on which he worked hard did not easily gain a foothold on the stage. Others were not rightly appreciated until long after he composed them, and several of them met with unmerited censure. Of the many operatic works I have touched on in the first part of this book, those which still live in our operatic repertory are : two comic operas belonging to his first period—*The Pig-headed Peasants (Tvrdé palice)* and *The Peasant a Rogue (Šelma sedlák)* ; then two works which were repeatedly re-studied, always with improved results—the serious opera *Dimitrij* and what the Italians would call the *semiseria, Jakobin.* Finally we must reckon as still living operas the pair of works dealing with popular legends—*The Devil and Kate (Čert a Káča)*, based on a merry tale, and the pathetic story of *The Rusalka.*

The Pig-headed Peasants and *The Peasant a Rogue* derive their librettos from a series of events enacted by typical Czech rustics, such as Smetana introduced for the first time in *The Bartered Bride.* In both instances the words are in· a light, colloquial style. The text of *The Pig-headed Peasants* is by Josef Štolba, who expresses in rather a dry and trenchant manner the simple and

8

natural incidents which occur in the story of the
pig-headed lovers, Toník and Lenka, who obstin-
ately defy their respective parents, betrayed by a
doubtful little joke on the part of godfather Rerich.

Dvořák's music is wholly in keeping with the
style of the libretto, which does not attempt delineation of character; it is bustling and whimsical, flowing in rapid figures and tumbling phrases
—robust and delightful music. The construction
of the various sections is very naturally carried
out and the music almost approximates to the
classical style by its crystal clearness. Although
everything is worked out with simplicity and ease,
there is no lack of delicacy in the handling. We
need only observe how finely Dvořák distributes
and develops the individual themes in the
orchestra. In the light opera of the present day it
is not the custom to work out the thematic material
so daintily! And we must remember that an
opera like *The Pig-headed Peasants*, which flows in
one continuous stream and so, to some degree,
links up its recitatives, *ariosi* and ensemble pieces,
was regarded as a very progressive work in
its day. As regards the individual characters,
Dvořák follows the librettist in sketching them
in very lightly. But the twofold style of the
libretto—partly rustic, partly comedy—is admirably carried out, and the leading features of
Rerich, Toník and Lenka are always transparent.
Although Dvořák composed this work with the
example of Smetana's *Bartered Bride* before him, he
knew very well how to preserve his own identity.

The Peasant a Rogue, for which J. O. Veselý
wrote the two-act libretto, is far more logically

constructed than *The Pig-headed Peasants*. The librettist makes use of the fundamental ideas of *Figaro* combined with *The Bartered Bride*. The Prince, captivated by the beauty of Bĕtuška, sets a trap for her, but at the appointed place of meeting he finds his wife instead of the maid of his fancy. The Princess makes use of the occasion to unfold another parallel intrigue, and tells the love-story of Bĕtuška and Jeník, whose parents will not consent to their marriage on account of the young man's poverty. They are disposed to favour the suit of the stupid, but well-to-do, Vaclav. The Prince extricates himself from an awkward situation, and promises the Princess to give Jeník a grant of forest-land which will enable him to marry.

The staging of the opera was exceedingly naïve and clumsy. The diction of the libretto proved very mixed ; sometimes excellent and then again rough and faulty. It is only superior to the text of *The Pig-headed Peasants* because it offers greater variety. Dvořák has taken every advantage of this, and contrasted the music of the peasant world with the aristocratic atmosphere surrounding the Prince and Princess. These, too, as well as the footman and waiting-maid, Jean and Bertha, sing songs which are quite cosmopolitan in character, whereas the rustic lovers, and the heavy and ill-tempered Vaclav, express themselves in the Czech idiom. It is characteristic music, which conforms very cleverly to all demands of the libretto. Above all, the lyrical and humorous elements are wonderfully welded together. This music is certainly all Dvořák's own, but in form and design the work—like *The Bartered Bride* of Smetana—

recalls the classics, especially Mozart. The classical comic operas of Mozart, and to some extent the French *opéra comique*, were taken as models by Dvořák here and in *The Pig-headed Peasants*; but except for the literary material and certain incidents in the course of the work, there is no dependence, musically speaking, upon Smetana. On the contrary, their styles are in opposition. If Smetana's standpoint is melodic, Dvořák tends more to the symphonic. Perhaps here and there he is inclined to spin out the musical texture to greater length than is desirable considering the nature of the scenes it illustrates. But, after all, this does little harm to a work so delicate and so valuable on account of its natural simplicity as *The Peasant a Rogue*. What does spoil the opera is the poverty of the libretto—perhaps the weakest that Dvořák ever set to music !

Dimitrij, that masterly work on a great scale, is steeped in the glorious mood of the 'eighties—that decade which saw the swift growth and splendid development of our opera-house, at that time our one artistic hearth and home. This opera is brilliant and festal. It won and held a place in our operatic literature. It was in vain that we were taught to see in it merely the reflection of French grand opera as represented by Meyerbeer, and that it was drummed into us that *Dimitrij* was grand opera only in that depraved sense, until we ended by believing it. To-day we know better.

We know first of all that the libretto of *Dimitrij* does possess features of French grand opera. That is its chief defect. The plot is based on the conflict between the Russians and Poles after the death of Boris Godounov—a conflict waged on behalf of the Tsar's heir by his sister Xenia and Prince Shouisky against the pretender Dimitrij and his wife Marina, supported by their Polish adherents. This struggle, to which is added the incident of Dimitrij's love for Xenia, and a series of subordinate intrigues, supplies many extended and vehement scenes which are somewhat motley in character and not always very true to the period. Nevertheless they offer a number of brilliant situations clearly put together. As regards the psychological basis, the chief character, Dimitrij, is rather weak. The contrast between the imperious and aristocratic Marina and the gentle Xenia is better drawn. Upon this libretto, written in good and musical verse by Marie Červinková-Riegerová, Dvořák lavished all the resources of his art. He snatched at this promising libretto, which cried aloud for a rich and glowing musical setting. In *Dimitrij*, Dvořák's melodic invention is wonderful. It contains melodies of such striking beauty that, once heard, they can never be forgotten. And the potency of his tone-quality is equally fine. He uplifts all the vocal parts by means of his inexhaustibly rich and highly coloured orchestration. The structure of the individual scenes shows a master of symphonic style. How wonderfully the work moves in great curves and with what power the scenes are built up to noble climaxes! Judged from the musical side, *Dimitrij* is one of Dvořák's finest works.

It is, however, equally masterly and important from the dramatic point of view. For this reason Dvořák was rightly attracted to the libretto. The

Slavonic atmosphere of the work is enhanced by his music, for he understood how to make the most of the contrast between the Russian and Polish elements. Musically the personalities of Dimitrij, Marina and Xenia are beautifully drawn in sure and simple lines. These characters have their leading motives, which are highly expressive and give unity to the whole multicoloured kaleidoscopic opera. We find also some admirable delineation of character among the minor parts. We need only listen to the old-world melismata of the song sung by the Patriarch Job, or the songs of the tipsy Poles. The warmest and most beautiful tones arise from the copious lyricism of the work. This makes itself felt as well in the noble choral numbers. These are extended to great—almost excessively great—lengths. But where the action demands rapid movement and animation, the music moves in conformity. There is not a moment in the whole opera when Dvořák's music is in conflict with the scene it illustrates ; still less could we point to a place where it sounds vapid or meaningless. On the contrary, the music of *Dimitrij* is always vital and ebullient as the rapid current of life itself. In it pulses a warm blood which removes it as far as possible from such lifeless puppet-shows as Meyerbeer's *Le Prophète* and *L'Africaine.*

If *Dimitrij* has anything in common with French grand opera, it is certainly not with its glaring defects, its bombastic inanities, but with its best quality—its splendid external effectiveness. This is self-evident.

Dvořák was deeply wronged by the exaggerated

censure of his declamation in this work. He never accepted Wagner's point of view on this subject. To him music does not grow out of diction. But to-day we do not take our stand so exclusively on the question of his declamation (which has been retouched in places) and, taking the work as a whole, *Dimitrij* proves that, in spite of occasional weakness, Dvořák's declamation is highly expressive. To-day, moreover, we are convinced that, even if German æsthetic judgments thrust it outside the pale of music drama, we should still accept it, in its strength and grandeur, as the issue of our own Slavonic flesh and blood. On this account it lives in us and with us.

Later on, with his popular opera, *The Jakobin*, Dvořák entered a field of work new to himself and to us Czechs in general. The libretto was again undertaken by Marie Červinková-Riegerová. The events take place in the old feudal days, and an attractive plot is spun around a certain lord of the manor and his humble dependents. Count William of Harasov drives away his son Bohuš on account of his too liberal social views. The Count's deceitful nephew, Adolf, manages to supplant the rightful heir in the old man's affections. Bohuš goes to Paris. At home Adolf has labelled him with the nickname of " the Jacobin." After many years he returns home with his wife, Julie. The old Count refuses him admittance to the castle, and he takes refuge with Benda, the village schoolmaster, organist and composer—a popular character in old Bohemian life. Benda, with Julie, visits the Count and pleads in vain the cause of his son. What the entreaties of the musician fail to effect, is nevertheless brought about by means of music itself. Julie goes to the harp and sings an old lullaby which her husband has taught her. It was the song with which his mother rocked him to sleep long years ago. The old Count is deeply touched, and becomes reconciled with Bohuš and Julie. At the same time he discovers the underhand part played by Adolf, who has always fed his anger against the exiled " rebel " and " Jacobin."

There is a parallel story which is perhaps truer and more sympathetic. It concerns the love of Benda's pretty daughter, Terinka, for the Count's young huntsman, George. The elderly Burgrave Philip is also an admirer of Terinka, but she cares only for her young lover. The rivalry between the two suitors gives rise to some delightful and lively scenes.

Both interests are developed in a series of incidents, now lyrical, now humorous in style. In both styles Dvořák touches the highest level of his art.

The prologue between Bohuš and Julie flows in broad, tender, deeply felt, melodic lines—it is the incarnation of the Czech lyrical spirit, which in the last act works yet another spell with the lullaby, " My darling, my world."

The sympathetic and beautiful characters, Terinka and George, are depicted in simple, sincere and human musical numbers—" Look in mine eyes " " In Autumn amid the Nut Bushes," and " In Thee Pain is Ceaseless." The amusing scenes with the Burgrave are frankly rococo in style and full of humour, with the drawling rhythms that parody the old beau, and George's outburst in the song of mockery " You know this Gentleman," with all its madcap, irrepressible merriment. Thus the chief motives of the action are underlined as it were by a suggestion from the musical themes.

The environment of the characters is one of the happiest sides of the work, because here Dvořák was quite at home. He, too, was a Czech music teacher and practised the choir of a village church. All his early reminiscences are embodied in the character of the composer and choirmaster, Benda. He must have drawn, too, upon his memory for the scene of the rehearsal of the serenade which is to be sung at the castle during the rejoicings in the last act. All is depicted with such loving care and kindly humour that the incident is classical in its robust charm and truth to the period it represents. This spirit of the old Czech musicians breathes from end to end of the work. It is an apotheosis of the Czech " cantors " of the past, a grateful tribute by the great musician to the teachers of his youth.

Both Dvořák's succeeding operas, *The Devil and Kate* and *The Rusalka,* were the outcome of his longing to approach more intimately the folk-spirit and to give his people a work which they would accept as their own. He once explained to the writer that it was his great wish to compose an opera which, like some of Verdi's works, should live in the people. The result is seen in the beautiful pair of works in which Dvořák has given a searching glance into the simple and transparent soul of the people—works which appear almost artless as regards workmanship, but which are wonderfully effective on the stage. This is partly attributable to the libretti which, in both cases, are better than anything Dvořák ever found before.

The text of *The Devil and Kate* (*Čert a Káča*) is by Adolf Wenig, based upon a folk-tale. The scene opens in a country tavern on the festival of the patron saint of the village. The sharp-tongued rather elderly Kate and her mother join the merrymakers. So also does Jirka, a good-natured shepherd. The music and dancing go on, but nobody comes near Kate. Jirka is obliged to go up to his sheepfolds. Full of spite, Kate calls out that she would dance with the devil if he came for her. Immediately a stranger, dressed as a huntsman, appears. It is the devil Marbuel in disguise. He is sent by Lucifer to inquire into the doings of the feudal Princess who owns the land. She and her minister have committed so many iniquities that they must be nearly ripe for hell. After conversing with the peasants and asking a few questions, Marbuel turns his attention to Kate and invites her to dance. Kate soon gets out of breath, but she is ready to dance with this fine huntsman till she drops. They take a glass or two, and presently he describes life in his " nice red castle." When Kate intimates that she is willing to follow him there, the floor opens, and the couple disappear together.

The mother's cries are heard by Jirka the shepherd, who has just returned from feeding his sheep. He volunteers to go down the hole and bring Kate back to her mother.

Jirka arrives in the infernal regions to find Lucifer whiling away the time at cards until Marbuel's return. Presently the messenger comes back in sorry plight, with buxom Kate clinging round his neck. Moreover, she has a little cross tied round her throat which weighs like a millstone on Marbuel and prevents the other demons from coming to his rescue. Lucifer finds her an embarrassing addition to his court, and the devils consult Jirka as to how they can rid themselves of this virago, who swears she will never return home without Marbuel. During a ballet of demons which follows, the shepherd succeeds in dancing her off the scene. Meanwhile Lucifer has satisfied himself that the Princess is quite qualified to become a denizen of his realm, but that her minister may be let off for the present with a good fright. To reward Jirka's services Lucifer instructs him to tell the minister that he has had a narrow escape, and to squeeze a good sum out of him for the warning. But if he attempts to save the Princess he forfeits his own life to the devil. When, however, Jirka sees her at the point of death, and so truly repentant that she is willing to set free all the serfs on her land, the shepherd is touched, and seeks a way out of his dilemma. When Marbuel is sent to fetch away the Princess, Jirka confronts him with Kate. One glance is enough. Marbuel runs for his life. The Princess gives Kate a handsome present and makes Jirka prime minister.

The libretto was well planned and offered Dvořák plenty of scope for his many-sided humour. In the first act, the shepherd's more lyrical part and Kate's racy comic rôle stand out effectively upon a background of sparkling dance rhythms. The scene in hell does not demand anything of a diabolical and sinister nature to which Dvořák's kindly humour could not have corresponded as successfully as it does to the merely grotesque suggestions of the text. Wenig's devils are really good fellows. A serious or tragic note is scarcely heard throughout the work until the last act in which the Princess comes in. It is a pity that neither the librettist nor the composer keep to the same high level here as in the two preceding acts. It is also to be regretted that opportunities for the clear contrasting of the lyric with the comic element are rather rare in this whimsical and multicoloured work, which, otherwise, is in the style of a genuine fairy-tale. One of the strongest qualities of Dvořák's talent is thus left in abeyance.

For the second of this pair of fairy-tale operas the text was written by Josef Kvapil. That is as good as saying that it is a poem in pleasing musical verse, full of tender, shimmering and shadowy moods, the work of an artist who was also a fine connoisseur of the stage and its requirements. Perhaps, therefore, as regards stage business *The Rusalka* is open to criticism; but its priceless play of emotions and refined versification satisfied the master that he would never find anything better suited to his purpose. Here were no elements alien to his nature.

The Rusalka (the Water-nymph) falls in love with a prince who comes to bathe in the forest pool which she shares with the old Vodník, or water-sprite. In order to win the Prince's love in return she is willing to become a mortal. The witch, Ježibaba, gives her a human body and soul on two conditions : she must be content to be dumb, and to face eternal perdition should her lover betray her. The Rusalka has her way, wins the Prince's heart, and is taken by him to his palace. But their happiness is short-lived. The Prince finds his dumb naiad a little cold and wearisome. He takes a sudden passion for a foreign princess who comes to visit his court, and the Rusalka is forgotten. She creeps back to her watery element. The witch tells her there is one way by which she can save herself, but the spell demands the blood of her faithless lover. The Rusalka refuses this way of salvation ; she would rather face her destiny and become a will-o'-the-wisp than injure her beloved. Meanwhile the Prince has discovered that his Princess is a heartless flirt. Filled with repentance, he seeks the pool where he first saw Rusalka. But it is too late, there can be no return to mortal life for her, and the lovers resolve to die in each other's arms.

The action is unfolded in a series of purely lyrical scenes. Here only the heart and its moods express themselves. The style calls for that warm and fragrant melody peculiar to Dvořák, and for tone-painting in deep luscious tints, with those contrasts of glowing effects and transparency of atmosphere which the composer knew how to conjure up from his orchestral palette. Open the score of *The Rusalka* at any page : what poetic feeling, wealth of melodic invention and sonority we shall find there ! The music is changeful, but always rich, and true to the legendary colour of the text.

Moreover, the musical treasures which Dvořák had at command are displayed above all in the great variety of these scenes. There is the atmosphere exhaled by the apparition of the Rusalka herself which seems to surround the whole work. In the foreground of the picture stand the lyrical scenes between Rusalka and the Prince—love lyrics sweeter and more ardent than any other which our native composers have produced. The first and last acts are particularly rich in this respect. Then, apart from the lovers, there is an element of the fantastic and grotesque, represented by Ježibaba and the Vodník. Dvořák has sketched the figure of the witch as cleverly as he has hacked out the outline of that most original, secondary personality, the Vodník. In contrast to these unearthly beings there is a mortal world of characters great and small : the Prince and his retainers, the cook and the woodman—a humorous quarrelsome pair. On these denizens of our world Dvořák has not spent such loving care. The scenes in which mortals play the chief part do not rise to the level of the others and are never quite free from convention.

In *The Rusalka* the master has been very successful in welding these various elements firmly together. This is a work in which we find that unity in variety which certain German arbiters demand. In the rounding-off and building-up of the entire structure on the basic motives of the action, Dvořák has achieved something organic and whole. The leading motives are distinctive, although not used on Wagnerian methods, and work their way through the whole opera, rising to the surface again and again, occasionally in modified forms.

In every respect *The Rusalka* is a fine opera, whether we view it from the standpoint of its poetic and emotional content, or from the musical side. At its zenith Dvořák's operatic work was distinguished as much for balance as for richness of details and complete unity of style. The same applies to the whole of his creative output of which I have written so far ; there, as here, he composes by preference works in complete union with his loftiest masterpieces.

Yet this music was only in some degree linked to the composer's life-experience. In the simple round of Dvořák's existence nothing extraordinary happened. A few tragic moments when fate, remembering this peaceful traveller on life's way, cast some fleeting shadows on the music which coincided with them. So, too, certain specially happy hours are reflected here and there, particularly in the brightness of some of the choral works. But often it seems as though all this music—like that of Haydn and Schubert—came from an unknown source. With all three musicians it took beautiful and perfect forms and was clothed in rare and glowing colours, although they were but simple souls, not very reflective and by no means calculating. Dvořák himself in his simplicity marvelled at his gift. Speaking of one of his symphonies, he said on one occasion : " What Richter found in that score of mine is beyond words."

This was a work in which inspiration only showed occasionally and emotion was given out only to a limited extent ; in which there was little nervous energy ; in which form and style were not

displayed by means of any highly cultivated
artistry, and intellect played a relatively modest
part. Yet it was a work which reflected some
strong impressions of life, although on the whole
it was the outcome of instinct—in short, an
extremely intuitive work.

We know that Dvořák understood himself quite
well. He spoke of his genius as " the gift of God,"
or as " God's voice." I remember that after
completing a great work he was always afraid lest
that voice might not be heard again ; lest the gift
of God should fail him, and the boon of his creative
faculty should be withdrawn. The intuitive,
instinctive, unpremeditated quality of Dvořák's
gift naturally had its effect upon his works. It
brought with it certain negative signs. Dvořák's
music could not be programmatic, for a programme
is always a refraction from the prism of another
art. A poetical basis to give value to music is
impossible without search and reflection. Music
weighted by a programme cannot well up with
the simple directness and elementary power with
which Dvořák's music flows from his soul. At
the same time it would be wrong to deny that all
through his career he was somewhat disposed to
programme music, then the most modern tendency
of his art. Still more erroneous is the assertion
made by some of his critics that he was unable to
compose symphonic poems because he was lack-
ing in the necessary knowledge of literature and
general culture. Dvořák's education was not so
limited as has been suggested by some who did
not know him well. If he was unable to write
programme music it was because by temperament

he needed no external stimulus, his soul being for ever filled with the echo of its own voice—" the voice of God." Beyond this no extraneous art existed for Dvořák.

To some extent this accounts for another negative feature of his art : its relation to the poetical text. Poetry, which is for many composers an aid and stimulus, long remained somewhat of a hindrance to Dvořák. But here again the insinuation of hostile critics that he could not adapt himself to the demands of declamation was entirely false. He understood this need perfectly well, and his musical conception of a text was admirable as far as concerned its entirety. But he could not always accommodate himself to the details of a poem ; " God's voice " could not always move step by step with mortal work. The stream of music which poured from Dvořák's inmost heart was not to be restricted to the narrow paths prescribed by the poet ; consequently it sometimes overflowed the verbal limits. Only by degrees, and after severe self-discipline, did he succeed in regulating the relations between the musician and the poet, and finally attained the desired balance.

The wonderful instinct which invariably showed the master the right way never abandoned him in the choice of a poet, or a poem, for musical setting. There is not a single instance of the selection of a text which would not conform to his temperament and musical inspiration. While reviewing the characteristics of his art, we shall have seen that he was guided by nature to national and popular material, to folk-lore and religious poetry. This

9

choice eliminated the discords between his musical inspiration and the poetical basis.

Moreover, intuition repeatedly guided Dvořák back to the sphere of his own special genius—to absolute music. Here he was in his own realm, untroubled by any outside voices, surrounded only by echoes from his own soul—echoes stored up from past generations, familiar reverberations of race, nationality and kindred.

Destiny worked a miracle in making Dvořák's brain the storehouse of innumerable memories of the Slavonic character. First of all he cherished features from the life of his own Czech people; and besides these, a series of brilliant, if less striking, reflections gathered from the whole Slavonic race. The preponderance of temperament and emotion over reason and volition is the outstanding characteristic of the Slavonic soul. Hence follow as a matter of course those mobile qualities which are tender and passive rather than aggressive. The Slav spirit tends to idyllicism rather than tragic conflict. The simple fact of " being " appeals to it in preference to glorious action; and even in action it inclines to the tranquil epic rather than to sensational drama. So it seems, at least, when we consider the special characteristics of Dvořák's art, and it helps us to explain many features of it in the light of his Slavonic nature.

But if we accept feeling and temperament as the chief components of the Slavonic character, we cannot ignore other important qualities: its elasticity and mutability. It may remain in an almost immobile condition, painless yet joyless, in a calm undulation like a hushed sea. In this state the

Slavonic "Dumka" is free of thought and feeds
only on sentiment, drinking in and lost in con-
templation of Nature. This is just the reverse
of Teutonic meditation which, though lost in
itself, is still oppressed with hard thinking. The
awakening from the quiet "Dumka" reverie is
usually very sudden. One slight external impact
suffices to set the quiescent emotion in violent
movement. Instantly the storm of anguish or
gaiety rages ; but the depths of the soul are rarely
agitated. Seldom such a tempest leads to a
catastrophe. It usually subsides as quickly as it
mounted. In Dvořák's music outbursts of gaiety
are more frequent than storms of despair. He
knows how to express gladness in all its aspects :
the quiet smile, idyllic happiness, boisterous
merriment, uncouth revelry. These fundamental
characteristics of the Slavonic temperament per-
vade Dvořák's music and lie at the base of its
varied moods. F. V. Krejči—not to be confounded
with the pedagogue Josef Krejči, Dvořák's master
at the Organ School—says in his fine and sensitive
study of the master : "His musical lyricism expresses the melancholy reverie of the vast steppes,
just as in his oratorios and cantatas we hear the roar
of the sea, the rush of mighty waters ; while the hot
blood of barbaric or semi-civilized races pulses in
his dance-rhythms." Krejči goes on to observe
that "there are two elemental sources whence
issue Dvořák's genuinely Slavonic temperament,
which gives imperishable colour and character to
his music : the Dance and the Dumka." Under
these two heads we may include all those powerful
movements in which his nature breaks forth, and

those in which his emotions seem to be in abeyance. All through the years of his creative activity, at least from the time when he penetrated to the depths of his soul, these two forms—the Dance and the Dumka — are significant and seem to have fulfilled his needs. Dvořák himself felt that the style of his music embraced something wider than Czech characteristics; therefore he gave to his chief work during this phase the broader title of "Slavonic Dances." The material of the slow movements of these pieces prove that here also he employs the Dumka contrasted with the Dance.

Another Slavonic feature of Dvořák's music is its religious feeling. His was not the deep, philosophically-proved devoutness of the German mind, such as we find in the works of Bach, which seem to leave the world behind them; nor had it anything in common with the God-defiant music of Beethoven, or the bitterness and inaccessibility of Brahms's religious outlook. Still less had it anything of the mystical ecstasy of the Latin rite, or of its almost theatrical pomp and dramatic gesture. Dvořák's faith was simple, humble, tranquilizing, comforting. It had some joyous qualities—it was even a little gay. Apart from its Slavonic features it is something purely individual. In the vast literature of sacred song, Dvořák's Biblical Songs stand alone. They have no touch of exoticism and no lyrical kith or kin.

Among the specially Czech qualities of Dvořák's music I am always impressed by his sane, robust feeling for the soil: " On earth's bosom I have grown up," he seems to say ; " our soil has nourished me and it will be my covering in death ; it is inseparably linked with my joys and sorrows and with the uprising of my most fervent prayers." The beauty of Dvořák's music is of this world— *our* world. He knows nothing of joys which derive from worlds of myth and phantasy; he does not seek exotic charms from unknown countries; neither does he soar into heights above sight of his native land, nor plunge into depths where the splendour of his native land might be eclipsed for him. For this reason Dvořák's music lacks something in breadth of outlook. His emotional limits do not reach into infinity as with Beethoven, or even to some extent with Bruckner. The poles of sentiment are not even so wide apart with Dvořák as with Brahms, but the world which lies between them is full of radiant and cheerful beauty.

A cheerful outlook on the world, what may even be called a certain happy carelessness, are characteristic of Dvořák. Nowhere in his work gloom predominates, never do we find any tract completely enveloped in darkness. Nothing in his music suggests insensibility, nothing dies out in deadly apathy. Light joy, vivid colour, movement, all predominate in his music. His works show all the signs of a life which knows joy and laughter in all their aspects. Dvořák's laughter, which echoes in his lively movements, and his humour, is Czech, and a leading feature of his art. The humorous power which conquers all hearts in his music has been rightly emphasized at home and abroad. But, here again, it is a quality which differs essentially from German humour, which is sometimes uncouth and occasionally malicious, ironical or baneful. It differs, too, from Latin humour,

with its wit and polished charm. Dvořák's humour
is good-hearted, roguish and harmless. However
biting and pithy Czech humour may be at times,
whether wild and unbridled, or mild and wreathed
in tender smiles, it always has the characteristics
of Slavonic humour, its freshness and irresistible
frankness.

Dvořák's indisputable link with Czech rural
music may be attributed to the fact that his youth
was spent in country surroundings. His father
came of a family of village musicians, and his son
also spent many an evening at the desk, violin
or viola in hand. It is not surprising that years
afterwards long-lost and forgotten dance rhythms
came back to him, and that his memory was
flooded with the characteristic accent of the
"furiant." Nor can we wonder that certain
peculiarities of rustic instrumentation (such as
the false entry of the trumpet) should wantonly
disturb his harmony, or that certain turns of
figuration should reappear in idealized forms long
afterwards. Again and again we find Dvořák
recurring to the idealization of the dance-rhythms
which enlivened his youth. Probably he drew
upon them, as from some secret source, for the
rhythmic power which lives with such intensity in
his music. This, and other less purely racial and
national characteristics, influence both the content
and, to some extent, the form of Dvořák's compositions.

Naturally, seeing Dvořák's protracted development and the great volume of his music, these
peculiarities are not equally marked in all his
works. The contents of his compositions vary

considerably. They are not always derived from his deepest inner feelings ; the · " voice within " does not always speak with the same force and eloquence. Some of his works are merely " Spielmusik," as the Germans say—a play of sounds only slightly connected with his inmost soul. Above all, this applies to his various dances for pianoforte —minuets, mazurkas, valses, and to the Suite for Piano in A major (Op. 98), as well as to some of the lighter chamber music : the Serenades, the String Quintet in G, the Bagatelles for Two Violins, 'Cello and Harmonium, the String Trio with Viola, the Sonatinas for Viola—all of which may be accepted as belonging to the category of his lighter style.

In the compositions constructed on a broader basis, the note of force and fulness is heard. The subject-matter of Dvořák's works changes with the course of time and grows loftier with his continual development. He overcame his youthful sentimentality very early ; extreme subjectivity only hindered him for a short time. In few of his works does he speak of himself. Soon the Czech and Slavonic world opened its doors to him, and, after that, the racial element developed and gave greater strength, virility, depth and warmth to his music. And yet, with the coming of the increased clarity and tranquillity which mark the later years of his career, nothing of youthful beauty is lost. The fire of earlier years is not extinguished ; it burns more quietly, but with undiminished glow, even in the master's last works. " The voice of God " continued to make itself heard, and " the gift of God " was not taken from him. Dvořák, who was technically mature at an early stage of his life, preserved his youthful freshness of emotion until the end of his days.

Thus the master's work may be briefly estimated, and his identity, as represented in absolute music, may be understood.

There remains the sum-total of his activities to be fixed before we can deduce his importance as a musician, at once so simple and so individual. We have passed in review the great bulk of Dvořák's output. Several lesser compositions have been tacitly overlooked, but, even so, a good deal of important material has had to be omitted.

If we judge him by the extent of his work only, Dvořák is incontestably a phenomenon in music. In this respect he approaches the copiousness of the great classical masters, whom he revered as examples, and with whom he had intuitively much in common as regards the style of his music. We have seen, too, the extraordinary variety of his work. Not merely its striking play of colour, but the open floodgates of his creative genius. His superfluity of inward creative power, pressing upwards to the light, could not be restricted to one path, but made its own channels in different directions ; and whatever channel he chose led towards the sun. To-day we recognize Dvořák not only as the composer of absolute music, of symphonies, and chamber works. Even with his oratorios his activities did not end. His operas still live and are taking firmer hold on our stage, and the world, which seems to be breaking away from the belief that only in Wagner's works salvation can be found, may yet acclaim his dramatic art as it has acclaimed his chamber music. The appeal of Jaromír Borecký, who has reminded us of Dvořák's great importance as a song-writer, no longer remains a lone voice in the desert. It has awakened echoes.

In every sphere Dvořák has his significance. In each of his tendencies we may discover an occasional break or deviation, but he follows in the main the path of ascent and development which leads to organic unity of form. Throughout his work we see this spirit of unity—the Slavonic spirit, most frequently shown in its Czech aspect. Slavonic lyricism is the essence of his art whatever form it may take. He always discloses his soul in his music, and his personality is as original in the choice of subject as it is in all that concerns thought, invention and workmanship. The development of his ideas is genuine and complete.

From time to time doubts have been cast upon Dvořák's claim to complete originality. In music, which so frequently draws inspiration from folk-material, there may be an occasional note-for-note similarity between one theme and another, but rhythmic and harmonic treatment have a great transforming influence upon such melodic ideas. The musical dilettante has always found a harmless pleasure in hunting for plagiarisms. We must bear in mind, however, that in all probability no work exists which is so absolutely original that it shows no relationship whatsoever—in idea or phraseology—to the music of the past and the present. Only, indeed, by such links it is possible to understand and estimate the worth of a new work.

It is true that we value a work more highly

according to the worth and weight of the new values which it links to those of the past. And we value it even more when the artist has succeeded in assimilating these values and imparting to them his own personality. In writing of Dvořák I have often referred to Beethoven, Schubert and Brahms. Undoubtedly there is a strong connection between his way of thinking and theirs. Nevertheless, Dvořák thinks for himself, and always colours his ideas with his own individuality. We find in his music both light and serious forms, but rarely exotic ideas. The same holds good of his method of developing his thoughts. I have shown how in this respect he clung to past traditions, and followed his three guiding stars of symphony. But he borrowed nothing from them beyond the fundamental principles of composition. Perhaps it was just because he possessed this instinctive tendency towards the forms and workmanship of the classical masters that he secured the unification of his work on the technical side. He evolved his technique through the course of years, and although he occasionally changed his methods, he never deviated from the path of unity. For that reason Dvořák's music seems to keep a clear aim in view : something genuine and free from extraneous influence. If we compare the proportion of his forms and contents with the measure of his power of expression, we shall find perfect balance. I think nobody hearing one of the master's works would gain the impression that the composer was trying to say more than he could ; that his means of self-expression, his invention and technique, did not suffice to the inner content of his work—in short, that workmanship and feeling were at loggerheads. Nor do I believe that any one could carry away the impression that the composer had ever created a cold, lifeless, academical form. The master's feeling for the just relation between content and form is so delicate that it always distinguishes clearly between the slighter type of movement required for a serenade or suite, and the great and dignified type suitable to a symphony. He knows instinctively, without theorizing about it, that the matter and form must stand in correct proportion to each other.

Dvořák does not merely belong to the epigoni of the classics. His work is not even a reflection of that great period of German music which found such perfect expression in thought and sentiment that we call it "classic." Dvořák adopts the forms of that epoch, but fills them with new contents which are his own ; fills them with *our* feelings and thoughts, and employs Czech colouring. This material, which was so novel in European music, throbbing with the force of a race as yet unexhausted, so fresh and rich in its ebullient vitality, gives to Dvořák's work its right to existence, and guarantees its life and triumph. Dvořák stands in the circle of the most distinguished musical personalities of the nineteenth century. He takes his place beside Brahms, Bruckner, Tchaikovsky, Borodin and César Franck.

Because this material has brought new, regenerative blood into the old forms, reanimating and moulding them organically, Dvořák may be regarded as our Slavonic classical master, in whom specifically Czech features predominate.

This completes what I feel the need to express as regards his place in European music generally speaking.

To make Dvořák's significance to us perfectly clear, it is, however, necessary to determine his relation to the creator of our national Czech music —Bedřich Smetana. The difference in their respective ages divided the composers in life, but not so sharply as the party-politics of the day. Smetana, from the start of his career, announced himself distinctly as a "young Czech," whereas Dvořák—a quiet, cautious, conservative peasant— inclined rather to the old Czechs, among whom he found his patrons. Highly as Dvořák esteemed Smetana's music, they were never personal friends. Smetana's circle could not pardon Dvořák's lack of general culture, and made no effort, therefore, to bring the two artists together. To some extent they were rivals. It is, indeed, extraordinary that in the course of years these two great men should have been pitted against each other as opponents— the one as our greatest composer of dramatic and programme music, the other as the leading representative of absolute music—in even less flattering terms, a progressive liberal musician opposed to a conservative one.

Let us glance briefly at the component elements of their respective arts. If we find some opposing elements, we may also find points of agreement. Possibly the relations between the two composers may prove to be quite different from what they are usually described as being.

The fundamental idea—the kernel from which a work of art takes rise—is nearly the same in both artists. Both are melodists with a highly developed feeling for characteristic rhythm. But Smetana's melody and rhythm is restricted to his own personality and to the Czech character, whereas Dvořák with his wider outlook showed greater diversity in these respects. His music shows a more general Slavonic colouring, and an exclusively Czech style appears only from time to time, while here and there we discern his close affinity to his models, Beethoven and Schubert. Smetana works in a more restricted area, but his outline is always firm and original. Dvořák covers a wider ground, but his lines of demarcation are less definite, and occasionally admit an outside influence. We have seen how at the end of his career he enriched his style by the addition of elements discovered in American sources. Smetana's harmony is simple, but in its own peculiar charm it is perhaps more original than the far richer and more complex harmonic resources which the younger musician, Dvořák, had at command. In all that concerns modulation, however, Dvořák is superior to Smetana. Here the severe discipline of the classical school was of great value to Dvořák. Smetana, self-taught, stood in a very free relationship to the classical masters. The same observation holds true as regards counterpoint and the technique of compositions in general. Here Dvořák stood incontestably above Smetana. This is easily explained. Dvořák in these matters followed the teaching of the great classical school, which, in purity of definite organization, is superior to the neo-romantic German school to which Smetana inclined. The same with regard to form. For these reasons, Dvořák stands high, at home and abroad, and may be ranked among the great masters of Europe as regards form and craftsmanship. Smetana pays comparatively little attention to the externals of his art. He seeks the chief significance of a musical composition less in its outer than in its inner meaning—in its subject-matter. He definitely fixed the content of almost all his works—whether dramatic or programmatic—beforehand. Smetana planned for himself a life-task : to depict in music the soul of the Czech people in all its most significant features. And to attain this great and splendid aim he sought all his years for a new musical idiom in which to give form to this racial material in all its breadth and variety. Such was the conscious and well-weighed purpose of his whole life.

Not so with Dvořák. The guiding factor in his creative work was not intellectual power but the gift of intuition. Intellect, which in Smetana balanced intuition, was of far less importance in the case of Dvořák. In composing he had no conscious programme, but followed his inner voice wheresoever it summoned him. And it was well with him when he paid heed to it ; for we have seen that when at the beginning of his career he tried to follow Wagner and Liszt, and when later he allowed himself to be guided by extraneous influence, he was apt to go astray. Intuition, and intuition alone, led him securely and defined clearly the kind of work he should undertake and what should be its subject-matter. Intuition to some extent decided the question of form. Looking at his absolute music, it is difficult to separate the proportionate parts played by intuition and reason. But there is no doubt that Dvořák was as safely guided by intuition as Smetana was by intellect. Without seeking it, without conscious effort, Dvořák found his destined place in Czech music. He became the continuator and finisher of Smetana's work. If the latter solved the fundamental problems of our music, Dvořák instinctively solved those which lay ahead of us. He enlarged the psychological basis of Czech music, as Smetana bequeathed it to us, by the addition of other Slavonic elements. That done, he turned to those spheres at which Smetana had only hinted, and created a school of Czech symphonic and chamber music. In this way he completed the work of his predecessor.

If the spirit of Smetana, with its greater width and profundity, could not accept the Czech fairy-lore, popular at that period, as a serious foundation for opera, it appealed by its familiar simplicity to the more childlike mind of Dvořák. In folk-opera, particularly in *The Jakobin*, he seems equally happy when drawing from a source untouched by Smetana, but dear to his own heart. Finally, in the field of the symphonic poem, instinct led him to the choice of subjects derived from his own circle of thought and sentiment, and to such programmes as carried on, rather than rivalled, the work of Smetana. In his symphonic poems Dvořák composed a chain of works based on Czech folk-tales, but more modest as to content and treatment than the grandiose national rhapsodies which Smetana created in his cycle " My Fatherland " (" Ma Vlast ").

In both masters we may observe some quite opposite characteristics. Undoubtedly they differed fundamentally; but both were endowed with genius. We observe, too, that although Dvořák was by far the more skilled craftsman he does not attain to the lofty artistic standpoint of Smetana. Opposed to Dvořák's perfection of form and technique stands the greatness of Smetana's ideal. If Smetana is regarded as the rhapsodic prophet of his country, Dvořák's music may be accepted as echoing the simple soul of the Czech and Slavonic peoples in its essence, The one artist is rich, the other great. The one is endowed with a strong feeling for large gestures, clearly expressed; the other has a gift for meditation, for prolonged enjoyment and restful pauses. In contrast to Smetana, our dramatic composer, we may point to our epic and lyric poet, Dvořák.

Between these two great national musicians differences exist. But such disparities of temperament and method afford no reasons why in choosing the one we must reject the other. If Smetana found complete musical expression for certain aspects of the national spirit, Dvořák gave expression to other sides of the Czech temperament. The motto of the Czechs should be in future not—" Smetana *or* Dvořák," but " Smetana *plus* Dvořák." Are not both indispensable to the glory of our music ?

Naturally an artist of Dvořák's distinction left his mark upon his age and surroundings. His influence was the greater because he worked as professor of composition in the Prague Conservatoire, and, owing to his personality, which never attempted to do violence to the individuality of a pupil, he attracted many rising talents to his class. His teaching career was marked by fine results. This can best be judged by considering the condition of Czech music before Dvořák's day. Side by side with the lofty works of Smetana we find a few compositions which, apart from their artistic aims and contents, were unable to satisfy the demands of a high standard of style and workmanship. Organized and clearly cut work, and limpid instrumentation, were not closely considered, except in rare instances.

Dvořák, without any specially rigorous theorizing, instructed his pupils in what he regarded as the fundamental principles of their work. He taught them to select an idea and to develop it, to build up a musical organism. He taught them the art of logical modulation and, by constant reference to Beethoven, he showed them the value of an absolutely clean outline, and the way to vary their colouring—whether for choral or orchestral purposes. He wanted all his pupils to share in what he had to pass on to them, namely, his perfection of technique. This he strove to disseminate wherever he came across talent. He was quick to discern a gifted nature and knew how to guide it with an expert hand. He understood how to nurture a talent, even when it was inclined to be stubborn and revolutionary. Vitězslav Novák in his schooldays was a case in point.

Novák, who in course of time succeeded Dvořák in the school of composition in the Conservatoire, still teaches on his master's principles. The pupils

10

were not encouraged in prolific writing, but rather to stick to one work, revising, correcting and elaborating it over and over again. In such slowly evolved and continually improved versions Dvořák found the best results. Besides Novák, he trained Josef Suk (afterwards his son-in-law) and Oskar Nedbal. Among his younger disciples are O. Horník, A. Pisaček and Rudolf Karel. Each of these men developed in his own particular style, but all show their connection with the master on the technical side. If their works breathe out the national spirit which Smetana awakened in our music, Dvořák determined the direction in which the younger generation should progress. He impressed upon the rising talents of his day the necessity of examining and keeping pace with the technique of modern composition, so that they might hold their own among their contemporaries, as he had done in his day.

As Dvořák was ranked with Brahms in his generation, so also the most important representatives of his classroom, Novák and Suk, may rank with such distinguished contemporaries, German and Latin, as Strauss, Reger, Debussy and d'Indy. Thus Dvořák still lives among us, not only through his music, but through the works of his disciples.

LIST OF DVOŘÁK'S WORKS

PUBLISHED WORKS WITH OPUS NUMBERS

1. See unpublished works.
2. Four Songs; words by Pfleger. 1865. See also unpublished works.
3. Four Songs; words by Hálek. 1876.
4. See Op. 30.
5. "Sirotek" ("The Orphan"); words by Erben. Ballad for voice and PF. 1871.
6. Four Serbian Songs. 1872.
7. Six Bohemian Songs. 1872.
8. Silhouettes for Piano. 1879.
9. Four Songs; words by Krásnohorská and Hálek. 1871 and 1876.
10. See published works without Opus number.
11. Romance for Violin and Orchestra. 1876.
12. Dumka and Furiant for Piano. 1884.
13. See published works without Opus number.
14. Opera, *Král a uhlíř* (*King and Collier*). 1874.
15. Ballad for Violin and Piano.
16. String Quartet in A minor. 1874.
17. Opera, *Tvrdé palice* (*The Pig-headed Peasants*). 1874.
18. See Op. 77.
19. Three Latin Hymns for Voice and Organ. 1879.
20. Four Vocal Duets to Moravian Folk-texts. 1876.
21. Trio in B♭, for PF. and Strings. 1875.
22. Serenade in E for String Orchestra. 1875.
23. Quartet in D for PF. and Strings. 1875.
24. See Op. 76.
25. Opera, *Vanda*. 1875.
26. Trio in G minor for PF. and Strings. 1876.
27. Part-song for Chorus. (See also Op. 80.) 1878.
28. *Hymna Českého rolnictva* (*Hymn of the Czech Peasants*), for Mixed Chorus and PF. (four hands) accomp. (See Op. 58.) 1885.
29. Four Choruses for Mixed Voices. 1876.
30. *Hymnus* (*Heirs of the White Mountain*), for Mixed Chorus and Orchestra (originally Op. 4); words by Hálek.

31. Five Evening Songs; words by Hálek. 1876.
32. Moravian Duets, for Soprano and Alto. 1876.
33. PF. Concerto in G minor. 1876.
34. String Quartet in D minor. 1877.
35. Dumka for PF. 1876.
36. Variations in A♭ for PF. 1876.
37. Opera, *Šelma Sedlák* (*The Peasant a Rogue*). 1876.
38. Four Vocal Duets. 1877.
39. Suite in D for Orchestra (Preludium, Polka, Minuet, Romance, Furiant). 1789.
40. Notturno in B for String Quintet. 1870. (See Op. 78.)
41. Scotch Dances for PF. Duet. 1877.
42. Two Furiants for PF. 1877.
43. Three Choruses with Accompaniment for PF. (four hands). 1877.
44. Serenade for Wind, Violoncello and Bass. 1878.
45. Three Slavonic Rhapsodies (in D, in G minor, in A) for Orchestra. 1878.
46. The Slavonic Dances for PF. Duet, arranged for Orchestra. 1878.
47. Bagatelles for Harmonium (or PF.), two Violins and Violoncello. 1878.
48. String Sextet in A. 1878.
49. Mazurek for Violin and Orchestra. 1879.
50. Three Modern Greek Songs; to words by Nebeský. 1878.
51. String Quartet in E♭. 1879.
52. Impromptu, Intermezzo, Gigue and Eclogue for PF. 1880. (See Op. 79.)
53. Violin Concerto in A minor. 1879–80.
54. Walzer for PF. 1880.
54A. Festival March for Orchestra. 1879.
55. The Gipsy Songs for Tenor Voice and PF.: to words by Heyduk. 1880.
56. Mazurkas for PF. 1880.
57. Sonata in F for Violin and PF. 1880.
58. *Stabat Mater*, for Solos, Chorus, and Orchestra (originally Op. 28.) 1876–77.
59. Legends for PF. Duet, arranged for Orchestra. 1881.
60. Symphony in D. 1880.
61. String Quartet in C. 1881.
62A. Overture to the play, *J. K. Tyl* (*Mein Heim*), for Orchestra. 1882.
62B. Music to the play, *J. K. Tyl*, arranged for PF. Duet. 1881.
63. *Vpřírodě* (*Amid Nature*). Five Choruses for Mixed Voices: to words by Hálek. 1882.
64. Opera, *Dimitrij*. (See below.)
65. Trio in F minor for PF. and Strings. 1883.
66. Scherzo Capriccioso for Orchestra. 1883.

67. "Husitska," Overture for Orchestra. 1883.
68. "Ze Šumavy" ("From the Bohemian Forest"), for PF. Duet. 1884.
69. *The Spectre's Bride*, Cantata for Soli, Chorus and Orchestra; words by J. K. Erben. 1884.
70. Symphony in D minor. 1885.
71. Oratorio, *St. Ludmila*, for Soli, Chorus and Orchestra; words by Jaroslav Vrchlický. 1886.
72. New Slavonic Dances for PF. Duet, arranged for Orchestra. 1886.
73. "Vnárodním tónu" ("In Folk-style"). Four Songs. 1886.
74. Terzetto for Two Violins and Viola. 1887.
75. Romantic Pieces for Violin and PF. 1887.
76. Symphony in F (originally Op. 24). 1875.
77. String Quintet in G (originally Op. 18). 1875.
78. Symphonic Variations for Orchestra (originally Op. 40). 1877.
79. Ps. 149 for Chorus and Orchestra (originally Op. 52). 1879.
80. String Quartet in E (originally Op. 27). 1876.
81. Quintet in A for PF. and Strings. 1887.
82. Four Songs : to words by Malybrok-Stieler. 1887.
83. Eight Love Songs: to words by Pfleger. 1865 and 1888.
84. Opera, *The Jakobin*. 1888.
85. "Poetic Moods" for PF. (13 pieces). 1889.
86. Mass in D. 1887.
87. Quartet in E flat for PF. and Strings. 1889.
88. Symphony in G. 1889.
89. Requiem for Soli, Chorus and Orchestra. 1890.
90. Dumky, Trio for PF. and Strings. 1891.
91. Overture, "Amid Nature." 1891.
92. Overture, "Carneval." 1891.
93. Overture, "Othello." 1891.
94. Rondo for Violoncello and Orchestra. 1891.
95. Symphony, "From the New World," in E minor. 1893.
96. String Quartet in F. 1893.
97. String Quintet in E♭. 1893.
98. Pianoforte Suite in A, arranged for Orchestra. 1894.
99. Ten Biblical Songs. 1894.
100. Sonatina in G, for Violin and PF. 1893.
101. Humoresques for Piano. 1894.
102. Cantata, *The American Flag*, for Soli, Chorus and Orchestra : to words by Rodman Drake. 1893.
103. Te Deum for Soli, Chorus and Orchestra. 1892.
104. Violoncello Concerto in B minor. 1895.
105. String Quartet in A♭. 1895.
106. String Quartet in G. 1895.
107. Symphonic Poem, "The Watersprite." 1896.
108. Symphonic Poem, "The Midday Witch." 1896.

109. Symphonic Poem, " The Golden Spinning-Wheel." 1896.
110. Symphonic Poem, " The Wild Dove." 1896.
111. Symphonic Poem, " Heroic Song." 1896.
112. Opera, *Čert a Káča* (*The Devil and Kate*). 1899.
113. *The Festival Song*, for Chorus and Orchestra: to words by Vrchlický. 1900.
114. Opera, *Rusalka*. 1900.
115. Opera, *Armida*. 1903.

PUBLISHED WORKS WITHOUT OPUS NUMBERS

String Quartet, " Cypress Trees." 10 Love Songs. 1865 ; arranged 1887.
Dramatic Overture for Orchestra (composed for the opera, *Alfred*). 1870.
Symphony in E♭ (originally Op. 10). 1873.
Symphony in D minor (originally Op. 13). 1874.
Rhapsody for Orchestra (originally Op. 15). 1874.
Vocal Duet. 1876.
Six Choruses. 1877. " The Song of a Czech." 1877.
Polonaise for Orchestra. 1879.
Latin Hymn for Voice and Organ. 1878.
Valse for PF. 1879.
Eclogues for PF. 1880.
" Memories " for PF. 1880.
Two Impromptus for PF. 1880.
Vocal Duet. 1881.
Impromptu for PF. 1882.
Humoreske for PF. 1884.
Two Songs for Voice and PF. 1885.
" Forest Calm " for Violoncello and Orchestra. 1891.
" Two Pearls " for PF. 1887.
Gavotte for Three Violins. 1890.
Two Pianoforte Pieces. 1894.
Slumber Songs. 1895.
Song : to words by Sv. Čech. 1901.

UNPUBLISHED WORKS

Polka for PF. 1860.
String Quintet in A minor (originally Op. 1). 1861.
String Quartet in A (originally Op. 2). 1862.
Symphony in C minor. 1865.
Violoncello Concerto in A with PF. accompaniment. 1865.
" Cypress Trees." 18 Songs : to words by Pfleger. 1865.
Symphony in B♭. 1865.
Two Evening Songs. 1865.

Opera, *Alfred.* 1870.
String Quartet in D. 1870.
String Quartet in E minor. 1870.
Quintet in A for PF. and Strings (originally Op. 5). 1872.
String Quartet in F minor (originally Op. 9). 1873.
String Quartet in A minor (originally Op. 12). 1873.
Concert Piece for Violin and PF. 1878.

INDEX